2.43

DICES or Black Bones

illustration by Glenn Myles

DICES or Black Bones

Black Voices of the Seventies

Edited and with a welcome by
Adam David Miller

Houghton Mifflin Company • Boston
New York • Atlanta • Geneva, Illinois • Dallas • Palo Alto

"A Dance for Militant Dilettantes," and "Birthday Poem," copyright © 1969 by Al Young. From Dancing, by Al Young, published by Corinth Books. Reprinted by permission of the author.

"Poetry," "A Dance for Li Po," "Lemons, Lemons," "The Move Continuing," "For Joanne in Poland," "Moon-Watching by Lake Chapala," "The Song Turning Back into Itself," "The Dancer," "For Poets," and "The Offering," copyright © by Al Young. Reprinted by permission of the author.

"A Collage for Richard Davis—Two Short Forms," "Last Night I Died," "Some Pseudo Philanthropist Flits," "The Room," "Dream #6," and "Excursion on a Wobbly Rail," copyright © by De Leon Harrison. Reprinted by permission of the author.

"Evil Is No Black Thing," "Work It Out," and "Back into the Garden," copyright © 1969 by Sarah Webster Fabio. From A Mirror: A Soul, by Sarah Webster Fabio, published by Success Publishers. Reprinted by permission of the author.

"Poems Are Songs," copyright © 1969 by Victor Hernandez Cruz. From Doing Poetry, published by Broadside Press. Reprinted by permission of the author.

"Mellow," copyright © 1968 by Victor Hernandez Cruz. Published in Ramparts. Reprinted by permission of the author.

"The Meeting after the Savior Came," "My Mama Moved among the Days," "Good Times," "Those Boys that Ran Together," "If I Stand in My Window," "Admonitions," "Miss Rosie," "The 1st," "In the Inner City," "For De Lawd," and "Ca'line's Prayer," copyright © 1969 by Lucille Clifton. Reprinted from Good Times, by Lucille Clifton, by permission of Random House, Inc.

To Lois—who else

My thanks to Ishmael, who introduced me to most of the Eastern poets, to Tom Wittenberg, HMCo's editor, who stood by me through sickness, arguments and in health, to my wife, Lois for her typing typing, and to the poets who make up this volume.

Contents   vii

Kolas

Al
Young

De Leon
Harrison

Sarah Webster Fabio

Calvin C. Hernton

Victor Hernandez Cruz

conyus

Lucille Clifton

Glenn
Myles

Ishmael
Reed

Kolas

black poets come from everywhere, have been everywhere, have
    done everything
    as they will tell you
        Poets
           makers
               vessels
               carriers
poets rapping, cutting, singing
of love, of lust, of ambition;
of being black, pained, proud;
privileged
        to be all that, absorb all that, return all that

Listen to them and as you listen to them, try to hear the music
they heard

    These are *not* poems *any*body could have written, nor would
any poet here be pleased by such praise. Merely because each
line these poets write does not declaim the 'blackness' of the
poet in the by now highly stylized manner *expected* of them, it
does not mean that the poets are not writing out of an Afro experience, that is, black life in the U.S., which provides more
in common than otherwise. They are writing out of such experience. What may throw the pre-set is the diversity and complexity
of such experience, its richness, its variety . . .
                    all that talent was there all this time

    What passes for most criticism today is bad news. Baaad news.
Too shallow. Assertion, assertion. Ego-tripping at the expense of
poets. Too little scholarship, meaning too much ignorance.

    Our thanks to the forerunners.
Langston Hughes, Gwendolyn Brooks, LeRoi Jones. Hughes and

Miss Brooks for their production and the exacting standards they set, Miss Brooks and Jones for their teaching, their help to younger and newer poets. Etheridge Knight, in a poem of praise, says that Miss Brooks' verses "stir us on to search for light." Jones for his production and his courage. The one U.S. poet in this century jailed for what a judge said was the content of his verse.

And to those who created places for the work to be presented. Joe Goncalves with *The Journal of Black Poetry,* David Henderson with *Umbra Anthology,* Abdul Karim and Edward S. Spriggs with *Black Dialogue,* Donald Freeman with *Soul Book,* David Rambeau and Willie Thomas with *The Black Arts* quarterly, Al Young with *Loveletter,* Tom Dent with *Blkartsouth,* countless others unknown who with a mimeographed sheet here or there, a broadside, a throwaway, a small press or underground sheet provided a place. To Julian Richardson with Marcus Books in San Francisco where you can read and rap, and who prints your stuff cheap. To Hoyt Fuller with *Negro Digest,* now *Black World,* which for nearly two decades has provided a free forum for many points of view. And that open air forum the Pacifica Foundation stations KPFA and WBAI.

It is no accident that besides the musicians the earliest Afro artists to establish themselves were the poets, because poems are songs and Afro audiences have always been close to song. During U.S. slavery and for some time after, the Anglo did not permit the Afro to learn to read or write, so the Afro's art had to be transmitted by ear. And so in the poems that follow, the reader should be aware of music. Play some black music before reading, play some while reading, keep it in the head . . .

listen

It helps if we can hear the solo variations, the changes in "1½ seasons"

birds . . .   the kind we were

flew up . . .

to here, n.y. . . .

. . . or coat

to travel in . . .

i was at least that for you

then: a joke you kept . . .

listen

Idea behind anthology was to include a fairly large number of poems by not many poets, enough poems to give sense of what each poet is doing, few enough poets to be encompassed. (Note, for example, the considerable difference between the A. B. Spellman of *The Beautiful Days* and of the Orangeburg poems.) A book priced within the reach of students and young poets. What is needed is to get the work out where people can read it, react to it, where young poets can see what is being said and how.

LeRoi Jones calls Bantu artists vessels of God. These vessels . . .

Awareness of music and people, music in the head, in the body, the spirit; on the tongue—music; the kinds of things that happen to people
>   in cities
>   at night
the city, but sometimes looking out, back, like Patricia Parker
>   I followed a path
>   . . . it led
>   to marbles & jacks
>   & dolls . . .

or A. B. Spellman
>   remember when we were young
>   together baby & every day where fields
>   rolled out spring came . . .

Some stackings—for poets.
Countee Cullen's plaint: "Yet do I marvel at this curious thing/To make a poet black, and bid him sing!"
And Etheridge Knight's answer: "Pity is not for the poet."

Miss Brooks' imperative: "One wants a Teller in a time like this." And Langston Hughes' acceptance: If anybody's gonna write about me, "I reckon it'll be/Me myself!"

>   Victor Cruz speaks of "doing poetry."
>   De Leon Harrison *conducts* "yellow"

Lucille Clifton:

> children
> when they ask you
> why your mama so funny
> say
> she is a poet
> she dont have no sense

Calvin Hernton:

> I am a poet.
> It is my fist you hear beating
> Against your ear.

Al Young—"For Poets"

> Come on out into the sunlight . . .
> Dont forget to fly

Ishmael Reed uses writing poems as finger exercises for his novels. In both he demonstrates a strong sense of the absurdity in our past fictions, such as that of the heroic stature of the white cowboy. *We* know that the cowboy was Mexican. A vaquero, dig?

To paraphrase that sweet singer, e.s.

> Against our righteous day, which is not long,
> Sweet Bones roll softly, as we sing our song.

Al Young

A Dance for Militant Dilettantes

No one's going to read
or take you seriously,
a hip friend advises,
until you start coming down on them
like the black poet you truly are
& ink in lots of black in your poems
soul is not enough
you need real color
shining out of real skin
nappy snaggly afro hair
baby grow up & dig on *that*!

You got to learn to put in about
stone black fists
coming up against white jaws
& red blood splashing
down those fabled wine & urine-
stained hallways
black bombs blasting out real white estate
the sky itself black with what's to come:
final holocaust
the settling up

Dont nobody want no nice nigger no more
these honkies that put out
these books & things
they want an angry splib
a furious nigrah
they dont want no bourgeois woogie
they want them a militant nigger
in a fiji haircut
fresh out of some secret boot camp
with a bad book in one hand
& a molotov cocktail in the other
subject to turn up at one of their conferences
or soirees
& shake the shit out of them

Poetry

It is possible to rest here.
It is possible to arrive home
headed this way
thru the wind & rain of this night
alone
to a place where starlight
isnt the point.
It is true that we are orphans
under the skin
where fluids combine
& organisms function intelligently
where vision or sound
in image or vibration
need only be true
to spark the way there.
There is here & always was.
You sniff & clear your throat
in this unintentional night
borrowed from eternity
or let yourself be saddened by nothing.

I sit in a white kitchen
next to the young walls
yellow paper spread on yellow tablecloth
& scratch helplessly
wanting to take new leave
of the present
which was a gift,
longing to have known everything
& to have been everywhere
before the world dissolves
a tangle of journeys
& messages
unrecorded
undeciphered
wrinkled down into me

A Dance for Li Po

2 lbs bananas
2 rootbeers
4 McIntosh apples
(best of the little ones
which is all that was left)
orange juice
corn
halibut
2 dollars & something
a quick peek inside the bookstore
surrounded by the uppermiddleclass
housewives in expensive boots
hubbies in expensive beards
children got up like film urchins
in funny hats
funny heads

Al Your

The sky thickens
all the lights come on
I drag it all home
sniffle in the cold
cut across the playground
where kids're chasing after
flies they cant even see
wink at the inevitable moon anyway
have another go at the mailbox
exhale
take my place at the door
come in laughing at the musty corners
dig into the bag
take it all out
stack it all up
sing over the bananas

Stand there
just paying visits
to all the good places
Ive been over the years
trying out the different kinds
of darkness &
light
myself but a shadow
on the world wall
unpriced
unbought

gone today
here tomorrow

Lemons, Lemons

Hanging from fresh trees
or yellow against green
in a soft blaze of afternoon
while I eat dutifully
my cheese & apple lunch
or the coolness of twilight
in some of these California towns
I inhabited a lifetime ago

Hung that way
filled up with sunlight
like myself ripe with light
brown with light & ripe with shadow
the apple red & gold & green with it
cheese from the insides of
sun-loving cows

Sweet goldenness of light
& life itself
sunny at the core
lasting all day long
into night
into sleep
permeating dream shapes
forming tingly little words
my 2¢ squeezed out
photosynthetically
in hasty praise
of lemon/light

Dancing in the Laundromat
(or, Dust: An Ordinary Song)

I love you
I need you
you in the laundromat
among the telltale result
of the ubiquitous garment industry
shirts & blouses
(we have arms)
bras & the tops of bathingsuits
(you have breasts)
briefs & shorts panties skirts & bottoms
(we have bottoms centers middles stomachs
bellies crotches & cores)
on down to trousers & slacks
& contemporary leg gear butt-
lined whitelined bluelined
roselined blacklined khaki-
lined rainbow clothesline
line-up——

I blow you clean low kisses
from transparent lips
of vowel-shaped word
& no-word,
the well sudsed stocking-
feet continuing
the beds & sheets
pillowcases
tender towel & rag
apparel we take for granted,
delight of all but the nakedest eye.

What is it we wear
that never needs washing?

What is it we wear
that never wears?

The Move Continuing

All beginnings start right here.
The suns & moons of our spirits
keep touching.
I look out the windows at rain
& listen casually to latest developments
of the apocalypse
over the radio
barely unpacked
& hear you shuttling in the backgrounds
from one end of the new apartment
to the other
bumping into boxes of personal belongings
I can barely remember having touched 48 hours ago.
Jazz
a very ancient music
whirls beneficently
into our rented front room,
Coltrane blessing us with a loving presence.
I grow back thru years
to come upon myself
shivering
in my own presence.
That was a long time ago
when the bittersweet world
passed before
(rather than thru)
me
a vibratory collage
of delights
in supercolor.
It wasnt difficult becoming a gypsy.
At one end of the line
there was God
& at the very other end
there is God.
In between
shine all the stars of all the spaces
illuminating everything
to the two tender points

that are your eyes,
the musical instruments
of these strong but gentle black men
glowing in the dark,
the darkness of my own heart
beating its way along
thru all the evenings
that lengthen my skies,
all the stockings
that have ever been rolled down
sadly,
lover & beloved
reaching
to touch one another
at this different time
in this different place
as tho tonight were only the beginning
of all those
yester-
days

For Joanne in Poland

You are not to trouble yourself
with your ladyness
your blackness,
mysteries
of having been brought up
on collard greens
   bagels
   & Chef Boy-Ar-Dee

nor must you let the great haters
of our time
rattle in your heart,

honey
they are small potatoes
whose old cries
for blood
may be had
any afternoon of the millennium
any portion of this
schoolroom globe

from: The Offering

... And now Spirit
I give everything up to you
the whole shape the whole content
the light shining thru the perfect holes of my being
for I would live in knowing peace &
drink the seas the rivers the lakes & ponds
munch upon the natural earth & rock
of the plains & mountains
I would have you have it all
the achings the airs the bright mysteries
that flow from my eyes
like rays from planets
the sweetness of expanding space
tears & swallowings
the musicks that jar & delight
from the bones of my cranium
to the heels & toes of my awkward feet
I give it all up to you
the lies Ive told
the beings Ive killed
longings in autumn
eyes
structures Ive inhabited
dust of my languor
a tongue renewed
the precious sperm wasted in agony
under evening ceilings

cut off from alternate joys
my whole self streaming self
filing thru the dirty streets
pressing down grasses
rustling thru dewy screaming jungles
in cities & upon the waters
I cry crying fire
I sing singing thee
Spirit
from the blood
that connects me with
revolutionaries in exile
hungering mothers asleep beside babies
the fat cats in the offices
who would deny my brothers a journey thru life
as hard as it is
the cool movements of domesticated animals
moving on delicate pads of their feet
thru the fog of this day
on into the change
the so forth the so on
of gristle & bone sung
& played by flutes & bells
of the secret mind
Spirit
no mind
no pause
not a thing would I deny thee
in this blind twilight of my unraveling . . .

Pachuta/A Memoir

I too
once lived
in the country

Incandescent
fruits
in moonlight
whispered to me
from trees
of
1950
swishing
in the green nights

wavelengths away
from
tongue-red meat
of melon

wounded squashes
yellow as old afternoons

chicken
in love
with calico

hiss & click of flit gun

juice music
you suck up
lean stalks of field cane

Cool as sundown
I lived there too

Moon-Watching by Lake Chapala

> I love to cross a river in very
> bright moonlight and see the
> trampled water fly up in chips
> of crystal under the oxen's feet.
> ——The Pillow Book of Sei Shonagon,
>   10th Century
>   (transl: Arthur Waley)

IT CAN BE beautiful this sitting by oneself all alone except for the
world, the very world a literal extension of living leaf, surface &
wave of light: the moon for example. American poet Hazel Hall
left,

> "I am less myself
> & more of the sun"

                                                        which I think
upon these cool common nights being at some remove, in spirit
at least, from where they are busy building bombs & preparing
concentration camps to put my people into; I am still free to be in
love with dust & limbs (vegetable & human) & with lights in the
skies of high spring.

IN THE AFTERNOON you watch fishermen & fisherboys in mended
boats dragging their dark nets thru the waters. You can even buy
a little packet of dried sardines like I do, a soda, & lean against
the rock & iron railings but you wont be able to imagine the
wanderings of my own mustachio'd dad who was a fisherman in
Mississippi in the warm streams of the Gulf of Mexico. How time
loops & loops! Already I'm drunk with the thought of distances.
I do that look skyward & re-chart the constellations. No one to
drop in on. No one to drop in on me. It's been a long time since
Ive had nothing better to do than establish myself in one spot &
stare directly into the faces of the moon, the golden orange white
brown blue moon, & listen to the tock of my heart slowing down
in the silence. I can almost hear in the breeze & picture in the
sniffable award-winning moonlight the doings & dyings of my
hard-working father, of all my heartbroken mamas & dads.

WHO WILL LIVE to write The Role of Moonlight in the Evolution of Consciousness?

IN NEW YORK, San Francisco & points in between the sad young men & women are packaging their wounds & hawking them; braggadocios cleansing old blood from syringes & sly needles in preparation for fresh offerings of cold hard chemical bliss; ofays wasted on suburban plenitude; not-together Bloods strung out on dreams.

I'M OUT HERE alone, off to one side, in the soft dark inspecting a stripe of tree shadow on my moonlit hand, dissolving into mineral light, quivering donkey light, the waters churning with fish & flora, happiness circulating thru my nervous system like island galaxies thru space.

*   *   *

MEXICO CAN BE Moon can be Madness can be Maya. But the rising notion that we are in the process of evolving from ape to angel under the influence of star-gazing is the Dream.

The Song Turning Back into Itself

(take 2)

Breathing in morning
breezing thru rainbows
vanishing in my own breath mist
how can I still not feel
this warm beat of beats
my own heart of hearts,

myself: an articulate colored boy
who died lucky
who wouldve kept talking himself
into dying
creatively of course
the soulful touch

pulsing thru his nervous system
like light thru arteries of trees,

that mystified young man
whose stupidity knew no bounds
& at whose touch
gold shriveled to tinfoil
wine gurgled into faucet water,

a firstclass fuckup
who but for his Father's mercy
would have gone out of commission
long ago
would have been the original loveboat
cracked up against rocks in fog or funk

the rocks in his hard nappy head
the fog in his big blind eyes
the funk in his & everyone's blood
held in
waiting
waiting

The Dancer

When white people speak of being uptight
theyre talking about dissolution & deflection
but when black people say uptight
they mean everything's all right.
I'm all right.
The poem brushes gayly past me
on its way toward completion,
things exploding in the background
a new sun
in a new sky
canteloupes & watermelon for breakfast

in the Flamingo Motel
with cousin Inez
her brown face stretching & tightening
to keep control of the situation,
pretty Indian cheeks
cold black wavelets of hair,
her boyfriend
smiling from his suit.
We discuss concentration camps
& the end of time.
My mustache
wet with canteloupe juice
would probably singe
faster than the rest of me
like the feathers of a bird over flame
in final solution of
the Amurkan problem.
Ah, Allah,
that thou hast not forsaken me
is proven by the light
playing around the plastic slats
of half-shut venetian blinds
rattling in this room on time
in this hemisphere on fire.
The descendants of slaves
brush their teeth
adorn themselves before mirrors
speak of peace & of living kindness &
touch one another
intuitively & in open understanding.
"It could be the end of the world,"
she says, "they use to didnt be afraid
of us but now that they are
what choice do they have
but to try & kill us?"
but she laughs & I laugh & he laughs
& the calmness in their eyes
reaches me finally
as I dig my spoon into the belly of a melon

Birthday Poem

First light of day in Mississippi
son of laborer & of house wife
it says so on the official photostat
not son of fisherman & child fugitive
from cotton fields & potato patches
from sugarcane chickens & well-water
from kerosene lamps & watermelons
mules named jack or jenny & wagonwheels,

years of meaningless farm work
work Work WORK WORK *WORK*—
"Papa pull you outta school bout March
to stay on the place & work the crop"
—her own earliest knowledge
of human hopelessness & waste

She carried me around nine months
inside her fifteen year old self
before here I sit numbering it all

How I got from then to now
is the mystery that could fill a whole library
much less an arbitrary stanza

But of course you already know about that
from your own random suffering
& sudden inexplicable bliss

For Poets

Stay beautiful
but dont stay down underground too long
Dont turn into a mole
or a worm
or a root
or a stone

Come on out into the sunlight
Breathe in trees
Knock out mountains
Commune with snakes
& be the very hero of birds

Dont forget to poke your head up
& blink
Think
Walk all around
Swim upstream

Dont forget to fly

De Leon Harrison

The Seed of Nimrod

the seed of Nimrod
brings forth matter/

its movement
& the void

The Room

Lines Parallel

Traveling

at the speed of light
to disappear
under verticle
obstacles called walls

Invisible filling (air)
Not Restricting

My movements

Constant Molecular motion
I am Told
To give motion to a Stillness

Creases race skyward at given points
to give definite boundaries

I leave through a tear in the Paper
so as Not to disturb the rhythm

Nor realizing that without life
there is no rhythm

Dream #6

in the wall

        roaches pitter-and-patter
and I long to be among their ranks
        enjoying this filth

worms enter my brain through a
festering sore atop my head
        my nose bleeds continuously

outside,
    naked light bulbs illuminate
maseratis awaiting ownership
a long way from home

flag draped coffins parade by
in an endless stream of color
leaving trails of splattered blood
followed by little girls in black
with withered violets reeking

(two dancers leap gracefully out
across a wide boulevard
both are decapitated but continue
as if nothing has happened)

christ once again descends
and is caught in a cross-fire
between the FBI and me.
the bullets are not repelled
he dies heroically for the umteenth time

I listen for the melody
that will signal another scene
but there is none
        only the jangling alarm clock.

Excursion on A Wobbly Rail*

. . . while it is true that the nature of man
is that he must in some ways suffer
        i tend to view my suffering as
an excursion through the system . . .

        they say Simplicity closed today
                up 2½
                and for those who held there was glee

        and green urinals leaked at p.s. 32
                and for those who pissed there was
glee
                . . . . I do not choose to join you
                i wish to be left alone . . .

(now this will be interpreted as some witty poetic
wind pass which should be over looked)

        . . . why? . . .

        the poet is to reflect the system
                in sickness and in health
        and never what is non-existent
. . . (broad exposure at this stage of the game is foolish)

        and so to rescue this poet comes
        this thing
        riding the gutter's foam
        wearing a patent smile

        and it would scream

        the eyes

                the nose

                        the private(s)

* Title from a musical score by Cecil Taylor

there is no form

                    no craft

and i would say   FUCK YOU

(and it would cower saying "i can-
                    not re-
                    peat wha-
                    t you ha-
                    ve just
                    said"
and i being of kind nature would
repeat swiftly   fucku
          and it would flinch

. . . butterflies fly faster than birds
          (heh-heh)
     i know because I said so . . .

additional information on the above recommended stock is
available upon request.

Some Days/Out Walking Above

some days/out walking above

the sky

between blood/hurled toward
the moon

others are found searching

brighter energy levels
          natural levels
                    cosmic levels
          universal levels

          CREATION

Last Night I Died

Last night I died
but I did not sleep

Tears crossed expressionless dimpled
terrains

                        Pausing
Not even to gain that momentum
Needed   to ascend the
Valleys of the Nose or Lips

Some Sphinx rose
on a Mississippi delta
And I hung from its lips
torn

Friends I knew refused to claim
my guts
for burial

But under the cover of darkness
My mother
and her mother   cut me free

Last Night I died
but I did Not Sleep

Some Pseudo Philanthropist

some pseudo philanthropist flits
between texas and the district of
columbus via Walter Reed
    dictating
the future of some three hundred
million people
for a hundred thousand dollars
a year and oodles of vestigial
    prestige

while domestic riesling of this
morning's vintage
            flows,
as free as urine on a warm summer's
night–through my father's body
and I trip under second stage lights
as Ayler churns on

I shudder to think
that this mood is not indigo
and this rope is not taut
when I see some old
baggy pant merchant
standing in front of his loan castle
        saying
"Do money worries get you down?"

with my eyes sealed with last night's
matter
    and the glitter from the
teeth of his toothless liberal daughter
who said just last evening
        under surplus blankets
"Do civil rights get you down?
sometimes?
            A little bit?
Oh I was just testing your sincerity
                don't be such a nigger
chuckle, chuckle"

while down south my mother labors
        and doesn't chuckle.

Poem for Herbie Nichols

The evening blankets even
the farthest notes testing range
of those pianoless dead riders

I see you now straining to hear
and cursing softly

The ivory shadows holding your voice
aloft but too   far

like the uprights that have the real
jazz sound/ringing/

In time there is   black

It would be a simple, quiet triad of the tonic
with neighboring notes

somewhere a junkie's jones would crumble

Up ahead you shout "It's hard to hear
with Bud playing so loud"

A Collage for Richard Davis* – Two Short Forms

Form I

Valley Floors
                        trickling
some god cursed   to spew   slimy
                                                      mouthed
four curdling   streams   flowing   intrinsically
fast fingers
(phantom digits)
snowy pines   frozen ponds   stocking caps
laughing-moaning   building-streaking   slashing
pricking   distorting
autumn winds   browns   reds   yellows
pizzicato lines   double stopping   expiring
strumming quietly

Form II

(silence)

* Richard Davis is an outstanding bassist on the classical and jazz scenes.

Yellow

birds & sunlight
a piece for *bird calls , bells*   apprx. time 3 min.
          & *silence*

bells should be light tinkle or chime like to
medium ring

varied improvisational rest

Sun   [energy]   rays $\xrightarrow[\text{quantity}]{\text{intensity}}$ conductor $\longrightarrow$ creative process

conductor $\longrightarrow$ yellow

↓

[musicians]

↓

birds   personal
          sub-conscious
          (imagination)

words
      3 poets

Sarah Webster Fabio

Evil Is No Black Thing

1.
Ahab's gaily clad fisherfriends,
questing under the blue skies after
the albino prize find the green sea
cold and dark at its deep center,
but calm—unperturbed by the fates
of men and whales.

Rowing shoreward, with wet and empty
hands, their sun-rich smiles fuzz
with bafflement as the frothing
surf buckles underneath and their
sea-scarred craft is dashed to pieces
near the shore: glancing backward,
the spiralling waves are white-capped.

2.
Evil is no black thing: black
the rain clouds attending a storm
but the fury of it neither begins
nor ends there. Weeping tear-clear
rain, trying to contain the hoarse
blue-throated thunder and the fierce
quick-silver tongue of lightning, bands
of clouds wring their hands.

Once I saw dark clouds in Texas
stand by idly while a Northeaster
screamed its icy puffs, ringtailing
raindrops, rolling them into baseballs
of hail, then descending upon the
tin-roofed houses, unrelentingly
battering them down.

3.

And the night is blackest where
gay throated cuckoos sing among the
dense firs of the Black Forest, where
terrible flurries of snow are blinding
bright: somewhere, concealed here deeply,
lies a high-walled town, whitewashed.

Seen at sunset, only the gaping ditch
and overhanging, crooked tree are painted
pitch to match the night: but I've seen
a dying beam of light reach through
the barred windows of a shower chamber,
illuminating its blood-scratched walls.

4.

Evil is no black thing: black
may be the undertaker's hearse
and so many of the civil trappings
of death, but not its essence:
the riderless horse, the armbands
and veils of mourning, the grave shine
darkly; but these are the rituals
of the living.

One day I found its meaning as I
rushed breathless through a wind-parched
field, stumbling unaware: suddenly there
it was, laying at my feet, hidden
beneath towering golden rods,
a criss-crossed pile of
sun-bleached bones.

All Day We've Longed for Night

In this room, holding hands,
joining in the small talk, our faces
with other languid faces mingling
in the smoke-soft light dulling
edges of day's end;

The string quartet plucking
sad notes from our sighs echoing
beneath the low ceiling and tingling
on the crystal rims of our olive-drowned
martinis as we take smooth sips, aah!

And outside, on the veranda,
under the milky-way canopy
of night, where our high
dreams—sandman bound—bump
their sleepy heads, we know

Only through these dreams
are we ourselves: all that we
may hope to be, locked in
our day-long longing for night.

To Turn from Love

No,
I cannot
turn from love,
in affirmation,
with measured
finesse, like some
dull fuzzed cocoon
metamorphosing into a
bright-winged butterfly,
a tight-brown bud
transforming, with
sunburst halo, into
a chrysanthemum,
a five-o'clock
blossoming, with
daily gusto, into
full bloom.

No.
If I must
turn from love,
it will be with
the cadence of an
addict flinging poppy
from tremorous grasp
while retched with
the effort of breaking
the habit, or a
gravedigger turning
daisy-filled clods
on a fresh made
bed.

Back into the Garden

It's a hell

creeping back into
the garden, shedding
your badly worn skin,
starting anew;

worming into the
apple unrelent-
ingly until you
touch the hard core:

and always in mind
the thought and risk of
your being bitten
in two before

you've gotten far,
boring feverishly,
and all you've left
are split ends.

It's a hell!

But making it
the shiny seed's
your prize and
genesis.

Work It Out

(Shindig, U.S.A.)

Steeled
behind
big sounds
twanged from
livid
guitars,
they moan,
shout, jerk,
twist and
duck—

out of sight,
eyes fastened
to the
tough
beat:

bodies
spastic
as from
deep within
force
surges,

heads,
in concentric
circles
of satellite
automation,
orbit

shaking
tail feathers
they cannot strut—
peacock proud—
must contort
on wailing
crowd mad
stages.

They
work
it out,
this thing
they cannot
name.

Not knowing
if there is
a proper stance,
they publicly

fidget
in their dance
to ease
the terror
of the
unknowing.

Calvin C. Hernton

The Distant Drum

I am not a metaphor or symbol.
This you hear is not the wind in the trees,
Nor a cat being maimed in the street.
It is I being maimed in the street.
It is I who weep, laugh, feel pain or joy.
I speak this because I exist.
This is my voice.
These words are my words, my mouth
Speaks them, my hand writes—
I am a poet.
It is my fist you hear beating
Against your ear.

Fall Down

(in memory of eric dolphy)

All men are locked in their cells.
Though we quake
In the fist of the body
Keys rattle, set us free.

I remember and wonder why?
In fall, in summer; times we had
Will be no more. Journeys have
Their end.
I remember and wonder why?

In the sacred suffering of lung
Spine and groin,
You cease, fly away

To what? To autumn, to
Winter, to brown leaves, to
Wind where no lark sings; yet
Through dominion of air, jaw and fire

I remember!

Eric Dolphy, you swung
A beautiful axe. You lived a clean
Life. You were young
Then
You
Died.

Victor Hernandez Cruz

Mellow

& real red grass went around in 1962/year of driving
into highways/like shooting stars/1963 came sudden
disaster/lions shitted the tops of buildings/holes in
their arms/year of bathtub full of bricks so pretty
on top of police car/but lions were gone/into the blue
air/the holes & secrets of their heads/63 of burning
skin/ash black furniture sails away on garbage trucks/
but not cause of real red grass/the red trucks of big
men in rubber/taking their time/letting the people burn
halfway into 63/the stairs were cracking/the wind blew a
different smell/more heads went down/stories of big buildings & elevators/with clean ladies of desire/cocaine falling out of their walls/willi bobo on timbales/the bangs
made circles/indians came with colors/painted warriors/
64 of pregnant girls/morning mothers hanging out of doors/
exchange hands/fast/

> at the market you make a turn
> a great event/

> the turn of floating/of
sky rockets & missiles/bright yellow smoke/music lifted &
glued to everything/iron & cement/bounce off wood/of glass
off of silver/

> riding thru the air/lips bubbling nonsense/
eyelids tear out/64 goes/

> 65 came in cars/& baby boys/in
anti-poverty jokes/newly high girls vomiting the dance
posters/middle aged men cut in half/at the peak of their
bravery/at their hottest point/65 of rains/leaning against
the wall/the sofa soft/cotton clouds/blinking eyes/like
windows/staring out at a lone fire/floating high in the
black emptiness/lost/mellow forever.

The Story of the Zeros

zero
zero
zero

    the museum of modern art/is zero ugly cans
    & piles & piles that eguel anglo zeros
    zero can O soup & O how wonderful the lady
    said about a geometric business machine
    zeroness is her/her empty zeros/the zero
    film the crowd made ape sounds & vomitted
    their chairs /as they spoke later about how
    some zero would egual some other zero/also
    others zeroness compared with another zero
    ness/it was zeros talking zeros/& about other
    zeros doing zero things/around zeros/things
    that came from computer & IBM /zero said to
     zero what about his latest film O its
    really his best do you not think/O & she was
    such a good actress/hehehehahhah rowa ro wa
    rawaraaraaaaaawaaaraaaratraooooo/the zeros
    walk from can to can from zero to zero to
    zero within zero/in the zero building of zeros
    & some zeros try to become 1/2 but they are
    the biggest zeros/within zero books/some zero
    said they going to write book on zero culture/
    the amount of zeroness in the modern novel/or
    de developement of zeroism in poetry/or zero
    play/& how zeros went to puerto rico & tried
    to add up/& how zeros went to sao paulo &
    tried to do the rumba/how they went to nairobi
    & tried to give some rice/& to/da nang searching
    for weird things to get into/but all them zeros
    did was to become bigger zeros & uselessness
    & de museum started raining dollars & all de
    zeros tried to get one.

The Electric Cop

this guy on t.v.
who rob everything he got
who rob
a thief
who rob
who kill
a killer who kills
this guy on t.v.

what they say & do/captain america tears his panties
as he swings for freedom

& ch.4 where they did
the rub
the two old men

what they say
this man
who likes pig a low
on your ass
your eyes dropping blood
will sell you some
cigars of death
for you
for you

the other ch. say you
have bad breath
& yellow teeth
something about some paste
& the guy zombie looking
&
this other guy
O he could kick ass
look at him pull out his 32/bang bang bodies
crash to the ground

planes fly/fire coming out of them
people scream democrats stomp
on heads on their way to meetings
cowboys kill indians
in their soft nights
& blond angels smile gleem brith teeth
put there by plaster of paris
young white boys run the shit out of their
femalemess/pushing tootie roll thru the air
their freckles tell us stories

the parade of
colors on t.v.
from ch. to ch.
round & round
the whole dial
from vomiting shit/to more b.s./an open
window of lies
& true stories of the empire/the end for instance.

Poetry Lesson

poem
like be an
old time
i mean
an old time
kicking ass
jitter
jitter
jitter
head stomping
jitter
jitter
jitter
ass kicking
ass kicking
along

along
ass kicking
jitter
knife swinging
crazy poems
crazy poems
crazy poems
like an old
time jitter
jitter
jitter
doing in
doing in
teeth & skull
like an old
time jitter
bug
jitter bug
poems
jitterbugging
poems
jitterbugging poems
building knock
ing down
knocking down
building poems
poem
is a pushing
aside
out of the way
like an old
time
jitterbug.

The Trip

No shit. The brothers went out like that. & who made it to
school. Be looking for you/who did. lucky. go ahead.
cause July is the month of goodies. can you see us/up trees/
into that anti-poverty bus trip. take over national parks.
shoot down the deer/the man said it against the law.
Night. Only place you can see the stars like that. are they
the same ones. the fire will cook us some grits. people
yelling from them trees. hey what you doing to them girls,
sticking them in the trees.
Americans on the highway look sick.
they ass must be shit/anyhow we threw stones at them. broke
windows. Splash into their eyes. Oh my god/one said. giggles
came from the trees. What a nightmare, one ran out his car
screaming. Hey be cool you guys. the night has wings/running
thru darkness & into trees.
The counselor said he coming for you cats.
let him come here & we'll hit him with logs & bury him
alive.
the night was cold.
Morning somebody stole the bread. Which one of you stole
the bread.
Fuck the bread are the eggs & shit still there.
Counselor: we got to be out by 1 0 clock, no body get
lost.
at 1 0 clock everyone was missing/social workers caught
fit. those niggers & spics are out in the hills smoking
pot/i know their kind.
the bus departed at four/on it were a lot of things that were
suppose to stay likeswimming equipment.
Americans thought the bus load was moving in on their blocks/&
probably registered thoughts of moving.
but the bus went on thru bridges & highways. & we/& we sang
boogaloo.
BOOGALOO BOOGALOO DEL GRAND COMBO.

The May 29th Fool

the city is rain
as we walk to fools house
nice suave fag with millions
gives thousands to take off of
taxes
    liberal fingers
spill red wine
              cookies with
gold insides
           how darling
the old man of popping chest
but who knows
             white man took
manhattan on a gip deal
                white
men burn the people of the
planet
the fool & sweet words
harmonize a new death
as rain bothers our eyes
ducking cars/& drops of rain

& old fools day
who knows
when we got to kick his ass/

The Dance of the Eight Ways

oriental bullet dodging
dance the eight ways of life
kick eight people in the head
yellow juice of speed
take care
spider man turn faggot & his speed
machine breaks down
body flying knuckles frying
bullets trying
dance the 8 ways
or bullets drying/

from *Doing Poetry*

poems are songs. poems cry & laugh.
a poet is in the world/the world is in the poet. things
are in the world. rock is hard/you better believe me.
slam a rock against your face. you see.
where they come from is where the poet was/the poet
was there/or the poem grew out of mind/but the mind of
the poet is there.
EXPERIENCE
poet records his life/his love of life.
his woman is a poem/& what they do together can if the
poem wants be poetry. or it's poetry all the time.
words are what the poet uses/he bounces words to
sing his feelings.
in the world the poet goes thru fire & ice.

thru ugly ugly cuts/or beautiful dreams.
burning yellow bodies is part of present american every-
day life.
dead indians on t.v. is common.

these are respectable things (situations or perfect happenings
there are poets of these respectable things. they write
poems about it. how they like to kill people.
kill being a good four letter word.

poets go in & out of worlds/people are in the world.

met a woman on 72nd street & she is fine.
or saw a picture of dead people.
or the Paxton Brothers put swords thru indian women
with their babies in their arms.

the poet sees & hears the world. & there are many worlds.

people live in different worlds (got different bags)
humans talk/dance & make noise/a poet must make poetry out
of that/or make poetry out his mind/which took form from
the world.
words & music travel.
god would not make anything bad or dirty. some people
make dirty things happen tho.
i see what's in the world & sing it
like god.

conyus

I Rode with Geronimo

I rode with Geronimo
I took Custer's scalp

I am the Scottsboro boys
I went with Robeson to Europe

I am the hand reaching/ for bread and soup in the 30's
I was the peasant—shot down   by Franco

I was the back held taut for slave whips
I suffocated in the bow of your slave ship
I died——— (with Emmet Till
at the bottom of the Mississippi)

I fried in the ovens of Buchenwald
I'm the lament
of ten million Jews
echoed throughout concentration camps

I'm the soldier of a thousand wars
fighting around the world   dying lonely
on foreign soils   forgotten

I'm Garcia Lorca
pointing defiant fingers at Spanish brigades
& dancing wildly   with Gypsies to the music
of flamenco guitars and lonely ballads

I am President Kennedy
bleeding in the arms   of his country
wondering   what happen/

I'm Bessie Smith, Billie Holiday
winging blues to Christ
him
on his cross
nodding his head

I am the soul of the people:
I'm the scapegoat of my country——
I'm the bleeding lamb of the world

I'm the wino eyes red reeking reeling
in the doorway of some decayed tenement
clutching his liquid fantasy

I am my Black brothers
searching high atop coconut palms
for manhood   lost in a shuffle
of white egret feathers

I am my mother
being raped in the corn fields of Georgia
Topsy is my sister,
Stepin Fetchit my brother
Uncle Tom & Aunt Jemima my kin——

Trujillo killed my father/
I picked cotton to send lily white
girls through college

I am Harlem
black bottom of an ivory top
Watts
burning hair of a mangy scalp

I'm the riot running through the streets
throwing bricks   setting fires   looting stores
taken lives—
given lives—

I am the wail the wind brings to you at night—
the increase in your stocks
your hemorrhoid problem
the reason you hate yourself
I force you to the suburbs
I make you sweat

I'm the tired body of Malcolm
resting——
thirsty blood oozing
from the loopholes of America

In the night dreams
of a young Negro child
ending certainly before the early sunrise

I am the ghost of Charlie Parker
riding the junky nod
to heaven & preaching hell
with monotones of alto sweetness

     I'm the phantom
     of a thousand lynchings
     motionless
     waiting in the draperies
     like a senile butler
to appear in a third rate mystery & murder my oppressors.

On Gossip Behind My Back

       Outward
The words slip
Forward like bullets from a machine gun.
      You a brave hunter
Of others feelings, strut through the streets
Like a water buffalo to destroy all matters that you can't
Understand all feelings that you never possess.

Inside your head a swelling tide of fears
Beneath your chest a dam of stagnant tears

A cool white iron burns between your ears
& hot steam spurts from your mouth.

A Gold Watch Hung in the Sky

A gold watch hung in the sky
A woman flowered me a son
I congratulated myself
On being so clever
& never took notice
That someone had put the watch in his pocket

Upon Leaving the Parole Board Hearing

deer feed on
the green slopes
in the
chestnut roam
of evening

spring again
faces me
beneath the bleeding
slash of redwood

trees in bloom
hollow bodies pendant
flowers in the moss

paths of sand
shafts of light
winding in & out
of shadows
to the summit

then descend
to the valley
like evening
ocean mist

clinging
to lost
horizons
i

Lucille
Clifton

The Meeting after the Savior Gone
4/4/68

what we decided is
you save your own self.
everybody so quiet.
not so much sorry as
resigned.
we was going to try and save you but
now I guess you got to save yourselves
(even if you don't know
  who you are
  where you been
  where you headed

My Mama Moved among the Days

My Mama moved among the days
like a dreamwalker in a field;
seemed like what she touched was hers
seemed like what touched her couldn't hold,
she got us almost through the high grass
then seemed like she turned around and ran
right back in
right back on in

Miss Rosie

When I watch you
wrapped up like garbage
sitting, surrounded by the smell
of too old potato peels
or
when I watch you
in your old man's shoes
with the little toe cut out
sitting, waiting for your mind
like next weeks grocery
I say
when I watch you
you wet brown bag of a woman
who used to be the best looking gal in Georgia
used to be called the Georgia Rose
I stand up
through your destruction
I stand up

The Ist

What I remember about that day
is boxes stacked across the walk
and couch springs curling through the air
and drawers and tables balanced on the curb
and us, hollering,
leaping up and around
happy to have a playground;

nothing about the emptied rooms
nothing about the emptied family

Good Times

My Daddy has paid the rent
and the insurance man is gone
and the lights is back on
and my uncle Brud has hit
for one dollar straight
and they is good times
good times
good times

My Mama has made bread
and Grampaw has come
and everybody is drunk
and dancing in the kitchen
and singing in the kitchen
oh these is good times
good times
good times

oh children think about the
good times

In the Inner City

in the inner city
or
like we call it
home
we think a lot about uptown
and the silent nights
and the houses straight as
dead men
and the pastel lights
and we hang on to our no place
happy to be alive
and in the inner city
or
like we call it
home

Those Boys That Ran Together

those boys that ran together
at Tillman's
and the poolroom
everybody see them now
think it's a shame

everybody see them now
remember they was fine boys

we have some fine black boys

don't it make you want to cry?

For de Lawd

people say they have a hard time
understanding how I
go on about my business
playing my Ray Charles
hollering at the kids—
seem like my Afro
cut off in some old image
would show I got a long memory
and I come from a line
of black and going on women
who got used to making it through murdered sons
and who grief kept on pushing
who fried chicken
ironed
swept off the back steps
who grief kept
for their still alive sons
for their sons coming
for their sons gone
just pushing

If I Stand in My Window

If I stand in my window
naked in my own house
and press my breasts
against my windowpane
like black birds pushing against glass
because I am somebody
in a New Thing

and if the man come to stop me
in my own house
naked in my own window
saying I have offended him
I have offended his

Gods

let him watch my black body
push against my own glass
let him discover self
let him run naked through the streets
crying
praying in tongues

Ca'line's Prayer

I have got old
in a desert country
I am dry
and black as drought
don't make water
only acid
even dogs won't drink

Remember me from Wydah
Remember the child
running across Dahomey
black as ripe papaya
juicy as sweet berries
and set me in the rivers of your glory

Ye Ma Jah

Admonitions

boys
  don't promise you nothing
but this
what you pawn
  will redeem
what you steal
  will conceal
my private silence to
your public guilt
is all i got

girls
first time a white man
opens his fly
like a good thing
we'll just laugh
laugh real loud my
black women

children
when they ask you
why is your mama so funny
say
she is a poet
she don't have no sense

A. B. Spellman

1 ½ Seasons

Remember when we were young
together baby & every day where fields
rolled out spring came, & longer days
full of sun & great trees that flowered
first, then grew so heavy with fruit
toward summer the branches broke under
birds, all kinds, the kind we were
flew up . . .
        to here, n.y., the great indoors
where winter with its funny habits finds us
cold & broken, responsible to the most tedious
snow, with noplace to go, or coat
to travel in . . .
        i was at least that for you
then: a joke you kept against the tedium of
those times that call the mind to reason,
what season & a half sustained you, the warm air
you kept around you . . .

The Beautiful Day #2

I wish they were invisible, those forces
white says keep him broke
& insane. they have the faces of buildings
older than the neighborhood. P.R.s playing
dominoes, chinese waiters, black southerners
just sent for, all the old jews, have those dead
junky forces in their faces, set as with old brick.

For My Unborn &
Wretched Children

f i bring back
ife to a home of want
et it be me.

et me be, if i come
back, new, hands in first,
he mouth in.

f hands & mouth are in,
he belly, filled, clothes
he body. *then* want.

f want & hurt are clothed, bring
back life to home. if
want decides, let it be me.

Sequel to the above

the whims of need, like
banking
accident
the wants of other people

pressure of
flood, of hurricane
wind in ear & all that
try to stay above it

you used to think i went
one way, you said a. b.
gretna lost a jewel
when you split

remember
we sang scat together
because we never lived
together i'm not gay

you used to drink & lose
your mind. they said no
unbroken glass was safe
when you were drunk

now you walk past home
& art to lodge a spike
in your left arm
not that i put down highs

but what strength that fellow has
he's all your blood now
his advantage is
he's not you

i worry for the freak
in you that liquor used
to turn on. i worry that
he now sits still to nod

The Joel Blues

after and for him

i know your door baby
better than i know my own.
i know your door baby
better than i know my own.
> it's been so long since i seen you
> i'm sure you done up and gone.

in the morning, in the evening
in the daytime & the nighttime too:
in the morning, in the evening

in the daytime & the nighttime too:
    it don't matter what i'm doing
    all i got to think about is you.

well the sun froze to the river
& the wind was freezing to the ground.
o the sun froze to the river
& the wind was freezing to the ground.
    if you hadn't heard me calling
    i don't think i ever could been found.

o i ain't no deacon baby,
i ain't never been a praying man.
o i ain't no deacon baby,
i ain't never been a praying man.
    but i had to call to someone
    you the only one was close to hand.

i'm a easy riding papa,
i'm your everloving so & so.
i'm a easy riding papa,
i'm your everloving so & so.
    don't think i don't hear you calling
    cause i'm coming when you want to go.

it's a pity pretty mama
that i go to look for you at all.
it's a pity pretty mama
that i go to look for you at all.
    but if it wasn't for the looking
    i'd be climbing up & down the wall.

Jelly Wrote

jelly wrote,
                you should be walking on four legs
                but now you're walking on two.
                you know you come directly from the animal famulee

& you do. but dr jive
the winding boy, whose hands only work
was music & pushing
'certain ignorant light skin women' to the corner
was never animal

was never beast in storeyville, refining
a touch for ivory on pool green
with the finest of whorehouse ragtime; use even
for the 'darker niggers music. rough', jelly wrote
but they loved it in the tenderloin.'

o the tall & chancey, the ladies'
fancy, the finest boy for miles around,
'your salty dog', but with diamond incisors,
shooting the agate under a stetson sky
his st louis flats winked into

aaah, mr jelly

John Coltrane

an impartial review.

may he have new life like the fall
fallen tree, wet moist rotten enough
to see shoots stalks branches & green
leaves (& may the roots) grow into his side.

around the back of the mind, in its closet
is a string, i think, a coil around things.

isten to *summertime*, think of spring, negroes
cats in the closet, anything that makes a rock

of your eye. imagine you steal. you are frightened
you want help. you are sorry you are born with ears.

When Black People Are

when black people are
with each other
we sometimes fear ourselves
whisper over our shoulders
about unmentionable acts
& sometimes we fight & lie.
these are somethings we sometimes do.

& when alone i sometimes walk
from wall to wall fighting visions
of white men fighting me
& black men fighting white men
& fighting me & i lose my
self between walls &
ricocheting shots & can't say
for certain who i have killed
or been killed by.

it is the fear of winter passing
& summer coming & the killing
i have called for coming
to my door saying
hit it a.b., you're in it too.

& the white army moves like thieves
in the night mass producing beautiful
black corpses & then stealing them away
while my frequent death watches me
from orangeburg on cronkite &
i'm oiling my gun & cooking my food
& saying "when the time comes"
to myself, over & over, hopefully.

but i remember driving from atlanta
to the city with stone & featherstone
& cleve & on the way feather talked
about ambushing a pair of klansmen
& cleve told how they hunted
chaney's body in the white night
of the haunted house in the mississippi
swamp while a runaway survivor
from orangeburg slept between wars
on the back seat.
times like this
are times when black people
are with each other & the strength flows
back & forth between us like
borrowed breath.

In Orangeburg My Brothers Did

in orangeburg my brothers did
the african twist around a bonfire they'd built
at the gate to keep the hunkies out. the day
before they'd caught one shooting up
the campus like the white hunter
he was. but a bonfire? only conjures
up the devil. up popped the devil from behind a bush
the brothers danced the fire
danced the bullets cut their flesh
like bullets. black death
black death black death black
brothers black sisters black me with no white blood on my hands
we are so beautiful
we study our history backwards
& that must be the beast's most fatal message
that we die to learn it well.

N. H.
Pritchard

As

WWWWWWWWWWWWWWWWWWWWWWWWWWWWWW
WWWWWWWWWWWWWWWWWWWWWWWWWWWWWW
WWWWWWWWWWWWWWWWWWWWWWWWWWWWWW
WWW   WWW
WWW   WWW
WWW   WWW
WWW   WWW
WWW   WWW
WWW   WWW
WWWWWWWWWWWWWWWWWWWWWWWWWWWWWW
WWWWWWWWWWWWWWWWWWWWWWWWWWWWWW
WWWWWWWWWWWWWWWWWWWWWWWWWWWWWW
WWWWWWWWWWWWWWWWWWWWWWWWWWWWWW
WWWWWWWWWWWWWWWWWWWWWWWWWWWWWW
WWWWWWWWWWWWWWWWWWWWWWWWWWWWWW
WWWWWWWWWWWWWWWWWWWWWWWWWWWWWW
WWWWWWWWWWWWWWWWWWWWWWWWWWWWWW
WWWWWWWWWWWWWWWWWWWWWWWWWWWWWW
WWWWWWWWWWWWWWWWWWWWWWWWWWWWWW

Aswelay

weary was when   coming on a stream
in hidden midst the amberadornment
of falls   birth   here near edge
            aripplingsoundless
leaves and eddy eyes withtrickling
forest   thighs   in   widenings
youthful nippling scenic creakless

in this boundlessvastly hours wait
in gateless isn't fleshly smelling
            muchly as a golden
on the crustishunderbrush of where
            no one walked were
unwindishrustlings mustingthoughts
            of illtimed harvests

            and as we lay and as
            welay and as welay
               andaswelay
            aswelay   aswelay
               andaswelay

above a bird   watching we knew not
what cause his course of course we
            lay we lay   in the rippling
            soundlessboundlessvastly
               of a firthing
               duty leaving welay
               wanting noughtless

               and then it seemed
               as from the air he left
               the bird who watched
               what would be called
               a dream

#

```
            z
           zzz
          zzzzz
         zzzzzzz
        zzzzzzzzz
       zzzzzzzzzzz
      zzzzzzzzzzzzz
     zzzzzzzzzzzzzzz
    zzzzzzzz zzzzzzzz
   zzzzzzzz     zzzzzzzz
  zzzzzzzz       zzzzzzzz
 zzzzzzzz         zzzzzzzz
zzzzzzzz           zzzzzzzz
zzzzzzzzzzzzzzzzzzzzzzzzzzzz
zzzzzzzzzzzzzzzzzzzzzzzzzzzzz
zzzzzzzzzzzzzzzzzzzzzzzzzzzzzz
   zzzzzzzz              zzzzzzzz
    zzzzzzzz             zzzzzzzz
     zzzzzzzz            zzzzzzzz
      zzzzzzzz           zzzzzzzzz
       zzzzzzzz          zzzzzzzz
        zzzzzzzz         zzzzzzzz
         zzzzzzzz        zzzzzzzz
          zzzzzzzz       zzzzzzzz
           zzzzzzzz      zzzzzzzz
```

Alcoved Agonies

Below
Cooper Square,
the January lateness
lies cold in doorways.
Men alcoved in agonies
sprawl
    their lives
outwardly upon
an inward
    World,
as if bottled
in a dream preferred.
Often, dreams (however
holy watered)
are unable to pass through doorways
like the cold of January lateness
and the anointed agonies of men.

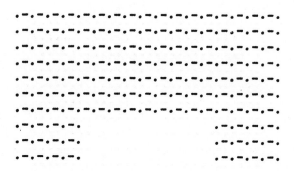

Parcy Jutridge

in thin where utters coast the light
few trace their mirrors on a fuel

OVO

```
00000000000000000000000    00000000000000000000000
0000000000000000000000     00000000000000000000000
000000000000000000000      0000000000000000000000
00000000000000000000       000000000000000000000
0000000000000000000        00000000000000000000
000000000000000000         0000000000000000000
00000000000000000          000000000000000000
0000000000000000           00000000000000000
000000000000000            0000000000000000
00000000000000             000000000000000
0000000000000              00000000000000
000000000000               0000000000000
00000000000                000000000000
0000000000                 00000000000
000000000                  0000000000
00000000                   000000000
0000000                    00000000
000000                     0000000
00000                      000000
0000                       00000
000                        0000
00                         000
0                          00
                           0
```

Etheridge Knight

To Make A Poem in Prison

It is hard
To make a poem in prison.
The air lends itself not
to the singer.
The seasons creep by unseen
And spark no fresh fires.

Soft words are rare, and drunk drunk
Against the clang of keys;
Wide eyes stare fat zeros
And plea only for pity.

Pity is not for the poet;
Yet poems must be primed.
Here is not even sadness for singing,
Not even a beautiful rage rage,
No birds are winging. The air
Is empty of laughter. And love?
Why, love has flown,
Love has gone to glitten.

Crazy Pigeon

Crazy pigeon strutting outside my cell—
Go strut on a branch or a steeple bell.
Why coo so softly in this concrete hell?

Fly away, dumb bird. Go winging off free.
Stop coo coo cooing, stop taunting me.
Find your pretty mate and let me be.

Like mine yours might be stone cold in her grave—
And mine too was pretty as a mourning dove.
Dumb prancing pigeon, mourning for your love.

The Warden Said to Me the Other Day

The warden said to me the other day
(innocently, I think), "Say, etheridge,
why come the black boys don't run off
like the white boys do?"
I lowered my jaw and scratched my head
and said (innocently, I think), "Well, suh,
I ain't for sure, but I reckon it's cause
we ain't go no wheres to run to."

Hard Rock Returns to Prison From the Hospital for the Criminal Insane

Hard Rock was "known not to take no shit
From nobody," and he had the scars to prove it:
Split purple lips, lumped ears, welts above
His yellow eyes, and one long scar that cut
Across his temple and plowed through a thick
Canopy of kinky hair.

The WORD was that Hard Rock wasn't a mean nigger
Anymore, that the doctors had bored a hole in his head,
Cut out part of his brain, and shot electricity
Through the rest. When they brought Hard Rock back,
Handcuffed and chained, he was turned loose,
Like a freshly gelded stallion, to try his new status.
And we all waited and watched, like indians at a corral,
To see if the WORD was true.

As we waited we wrapped ourselves in the cloak
Of his exploits: "Man, the last time, it took eight
Screws to put him in the Hole." "Yeah, remember when he
Smacked the captain with his dinner tray?" "He set
The record for time in the Hole—67 straight days!"
"Ol Hard Rock! man, that's one crazy nigger."
And then the jewel of a myth that Hard Rock had once bit
A screw on the thumb and poisoned him with syphilitic spit.

The testing came, to see if Hard Rock was really tame.
A hillbilly called him a black son of a bitch
And didn't lose his teeth, a screw who knew Hard Rock
From before shook him down and barked in his face.
And Hard Rock did *nothing*. Just grinned and looked silly,
His eyes empty like knot holes in a fence.

And even after we discovered that it took Hard Rock
Exactly 3 minutes to tell you his first name,
We told ourselves that he had just wised up,
Was being cool; but we could not fool ourselves for long,
And we turned away, our eyes on the ground. Crushed.
He had been our Destroyer, the doer of things
We dreamed of doing but could not bring ourselves to do,
The fears of years, like a biting whip,
Had cut grooves too deeply across our backs.

He Sees through Stone

He sees through stone
he has the secret
eyes this old black one
who under prison skies
sits pressed by the sun
against the western wall
his pipe between purple gums

the years fall
like overripe plums
bursting red flesh
on the dark earth

his time is not my time
but I have known him
in a time gone

he led me trembling cold
into the dark forest
taught me the secret rites
to take a woman
to be true to my brothers
to make my spear drink
the blood
of my enemies

now black cats circle him
flash white teeth
snarl at the air
mashing green grass beneath
shining muscles
ears peeling his words
he smiles
he knows
the hunt the enemy
he has the secret eyes
he sees through stone

The Idea of Ancestry

1

Taped to the wall of my cell are 47 pictures: 47 black faces:
my father, mother, grandmothers (1 dead), grandfathers (both
dead), brothers, sisters, uncles, aunts, cousins (1st & 2nd),
nieces, and nephews. They stare across the space at me sprawling
on my bunk. I know their dark eyes, they know mine. I know their
style, they know mine. I am all of them, they are all of me; they are
farmers, I am a thief, I am me, they are thee.

I have at one time or another been in love with my mother,
1 grandmother, 2 sisters, 2 aunts (1 went to the asylum), and
5 cousins. I am now in love with a 7 yr old niece (she sends me
letters written in large block print, and her picture is the only one
that smiles at me).

I have the same name as 1 grandfather, 3 cousins, 3 nephews,
and 1 uncle. The uncle disappeared when he was 15, just took
off and caught a freight (they say). He's discussed each year when
the family has a reunion, he causes uneasiness in the clan, he is
an empty space. My father's mother, who is 93 and who keeps the
Family Bible with everybody's birth dates (and death dates) in it,
always mentions him. There is no place in her Bible for "where-
abouts unknown."

2

Each Fall the graves of my grandfathers call me, the brown
hills and red gullies of mississippi send out their electric messages, galvanizing my genes. Last yr/like a salmon quitting the
cold ocean—leaping and bucking up his birthstream/I hitch-
hiked my way from L.A. with 16 caps in my pocket and a monkey
on my back. and I almost kicked it with the kinfolks. I walked
barefooted in my grandmother's backyard/I smelled the old
land and the woods/I sipped cornwhiskey from fruit jars with the men/
I flirted with the women/I had a ball till the caps ran out and my
habit came down. That night I looked at my grandmother and
split/my guts were screaming for junk/but I was almost con-
tented/I had almost caught up with me.
(The next day in Memphis I cracked a croaker's crib for a fix.)

This yr there is a gray stone wall damming my stream, and when
the falling leaves stir my genes, I pace my cell or flop on my bunk
and stare at 47 black faces across the space. I am all of them,
they are all of me, I am me, they are thee, and I have no sons
to float in the space between.

The Violent Space

(or when your sister sleeps around for money)

Exchange in greed the ungraceful signs. Thrust
The thick notes between green apple breasts.
Then the shadow of the devil descends,
The violent space cries and angel eyes,
Large and dark, retreat in innocence and in ice.
(Run sister run—the Bugga man comes!)

The violent space cries silently,
Like you cried wide years ago
In another space, speckled by the sun
And the leaves of a green plum tree,
And you were stung
By a red wasp and we flew home.
(Run sister run—the Bugga man comes!)

Well, hell, lil sis, wasps still sting.
You are all of seventeen and as alone now
In your pain as you were with the sting
On your brow.
Well, shit, lil sis, here we are:
You and I and this poem.
And what should I do? should I squat
In the dust and make strange markings on the ground?
Shall I chant a spell to drive the demon away?
(Run sister run—the Bugga man comes!)

In the beginning you were the Virgin Mary,
And you are the Virgin Mary now.
But somewhere between Nazareth and Bethlehem
You lost your name in the nameless void.
O Mary don't you weep don't you moan
O Mary shake your butt to the violent juke,
Absorb the demon puke and watch the white eyes pop.
(Run sister run—the Bugga man comes!)

And what do I do. I boil my tears in a twisted spoon
And dance like an angel on the point of a needle.
I sit counting syllables like Midas gold.
I am not bold. I can not yet take hold of the demon
and lift his weight from your black belly,
So I grab the air and sing my song.
(But the air can not stand my singing long.)

On Universalism

I see no single thread
That binds me one to all;
Why even common dead
Men took the single fall.

No universal laws
Of human misery
Create a common cause
Or common history
That ease black people's pains
Nor break black people's chains.

For Malcolm, A Year after

Compose for Red a proper verse;
Adhere to foot and strict iamb;
Control the burst of angry words
Or they might boil and break the dam.
Or they might boil and overflow
And drench me, drown me, drive me mad.
So swear no oath, so shed no tear,
And sing no song blue Baptist sad.
Evoke no image, stir no flame,
And spin no yarn across the air.
Make empty anglo tea lace words—
Make them dead white and dry bone bare.

Compose a verse for Malcolm man,
And make it rime and make it prim.
The verse will die—as all men do—
But not the memory of him!
Death might come singing sweet like C,
Or knocking like the old folk say,
The moon and stars may pass away,
But not the anger of that day.

It Was a Funky Deal

It was a funky deal.
The only thing real was red,
Red blood around his red, red beard.

It was a funky deal.

In the beginning was the word,
And in the end the deed.
Judas did it to Jesus
For the same Herd. Same reason.
You made them mad, Malcolm. Same reason.

It was a funky deal.

You rocked too many boats, man.
Pulled too many coats, man.
Saw through the jive.
You reached the wild guys
Like me. You and Bird. (And that
Lil LeRoi cat.)

It was a funky deal.

For Langston Hughes

Gone   Gone
    Another weaver of black dreams has gone
we sat in June Bug's pad with the shades drawn
and the air thick with holy smoke. and we heard
the Lady sing Langston before we knew his name.
and when Black Bodies stopped swinging   June
Bug, TG and I went out and swung on some white cats.
now I don't think the Mythmaker meant for us to do *that*
but we didn't know what else to do.

    Gone   Gone
    Another weaver of black dreams has gone

Cell Song

Night   Music   Slanted
Light strike the cave
of sleep. I alone
tread the red circle
and twist the space
with speech.

Come now, etheridge, don't
be a saviour; take
your words and scrape
the sky, shake rain

on the desert, sprinkle
salt on the tail
of a girl,

can there anything
good come out of
prison

William Anderson

There's Not a Friend like the Lowly Jesus

Suddenly, against the mountainous
wall of the fireplace,
soot begins to glow.

At the ocean
at that very moment,
the waves spread their lips.
In the folds of the sierra

nevada, a crowd
of skiers rides down the snow.
They hold torches, they
wave and shout, so you can hear
them in the
hotel.

If you're in any way
a prophet, you
better figure why a nigger
is different from yourself, or any

of the above lights. Because when I
think of all the things
I do to keep from

dying.

The February Rain Is Falling

Nobody can tell him these kids understand
political organization. He can't see why there's
so much dirt, both real dirt and sexual dirt,
in the youth movement. His face, his hair,
his eyebrows are white, but his eyes are
red from whisky, and the glass bead neck-
laces of his wife and other women in the
room reflect light from the kitchen. . . .

Telegraph Avenue, Thursday, 6:30.
We call the revolution to us when we please,
like women. The strikers come down
the street in a mass reaching from sidewalk
to sidewalk. The people at the edges
of the mass aren't as dignified—they skip
nervously, looking in back for the police, they
peel up and down Channing Way. Two or three
minutes behind, the police come like extermina-
tors. Tear gas shells burn brief and white
and the clouds roll like white wheels down
the street.

'Man, I like to celebrate Chinese New Year
as much as anybody,' says a Chinese student
to me, 'but this is taking it too far!' We grin
at each other, he jumps into the street where
five men push a stalled car, a blonde woman
hunching over the wheel. She is staring,
horrified, out the window. The Chinese student
helps push. The car rolls down the street,
the engine catches, the car scuttles away,
right through a stop sign, and whips around
the corner.

At eight o'clock the disturbance is all over
and police occupy all the intersections, talking.
A fat blonde woman in slacks can hardly keep
from patting the officers. A city water truck
is parked between Haste and Dwight Way. A

black man looks out the truck window with
a curious expression on his face—I can't read
it.

The street is shiny from water, there's a
faint smell of gas in the air, but store windows
aren't broken and very little damage has been
done. The truck starts up and streams of
water spray from nozzles. On the dark surface
of the street, the water spreads out like oiled
silk. A car rolls by, a black man driving.
He raises his hand in the clenched fist salute
and we grin at each other. I continue down
Telegraph. There are the Santa Clara county
deputies. I can hardly keep from grinning.
Two straight-looking students are whispering
behind me, 'Look at this. This will be history
some day.' No, no, I want to say to them,
we are history. The living.

At 8:45 the balcony of the Berkeley community
theater is half full for the last performance of
the Living Theater. Paradise Now. A huge
roll of plastic appears. Somebody holds the
core and the end is pulled from hand to hand
along the balcony railing, people shouting
in spontaneous pleasure. It's a snake, it's
over the balcony, down to the main audience,
zig-zagging with astonishing speed, twanging
against my head. I feel like an element in
a painting. My eyes are still smarting from
tear gas. Flutes begin to play. A paper airplane
floats down from above. The cast appears.

'I don't know how to stop the wars. I don't
know how to stop the fucking wars,' Rufus
Collins whispers in my ear from behind.

He is a black man in the cast. Other actors
appear:
> I'm not allowed to smoke marijuana.
> I'm not allowed to take off my clothes.
> You can't live if you don't have money.

A low moan immediately begins in the audience.
By now hundreds of people are on the stage
and they begin to stamp their feet. Many older
people in the audience look at the scene as if
they were looking at it through old glass, at
something horrible in themselves which they've
thank God got under control. Yet it is the same
kind of control that keeps them at their jobs.

The cast sit in a rough circle on the stage.
They're dressed in breechcloths, G-strings,
handkerchief bras, strips of cloth. The audience
is thirteen deep around them.
'Down in front,' yells somebody from the seated
audience—they are still reasonable down there.
'What do you think living theater is?' a boy
shouts beside me. The people on the stage sweep
into the small circle of the cast, dancing,
shouting, singing. The cast form, almost by
force, a pyramid in the blue stage light.
Members of the theater staff climb the ladders
at the rear of the stage and clear the catwalk
because there is an irresistible temptation
up there. The audience is shouting like bull-
horns, and the cast is screaming:
        ANARCHISM!   ANARCHISM!   ANARCHISM!

'What about the starving blacks? How do we get
the pigs off campus?' yells go up from the audience,
and suddenly political arguments are popping
in a dozen places.

'By love. By life. By the force of the revolutionary
imagination,' an actor screams, almost hidden
by the raging Berkeley young.
'Bull shit' shouts a student. An actress runs up
to him, sticks her dead white face right into his,
and screams, 'Fuck you. Fuck you!'

'If you're woman enough, I'm man enough,' he
screams right back. She glares at him for a
moment, then races up the aisle. A girl is

carried by, wrapped in a cocoon of plastic.
She smiles, she is comfortable. Part of the
cast is on the stage now, chanting, 'To be free
is to know where you're at. To be free is to be
free . . . to think . . . to feel . . . to act.' They
writhe, they grimace and stretch their arms
to the ceiling.

'You aren't even real people. You're actors,'
another student yells at one of the cast—both of
them are standing on seat arms, arguing
politics. 'Fuck you!' shouts the actor
and he tries to continue his argument with
the knot of people gathered around him.

'You're just TV washouts. You don't even
believe all this. You're just practicing,'
the student persists. At first his impossibly
blonde chick was trying to shame him down
but suddenly she grins, her eyes flare, as
if she were at a demonstration, and she climbs
up beside him, they link arms and prance,
precariously, still on the seat arms. They
grab the actor's hand and jerk him into the
rhythm of their satire. He's still feebly
protesting, 'We're all human, we're all
human,' but it is as if a high wind had struck
him. His voice falters as if it were being blown
instantly into the past.

On the stage a small group of people form a
love mound, kissing, hugging and touching on
the stage floor. One man has his knee
cleverly pressed against a girl's crotch and
he's trying to rub her up. She has a hand down
there to push his knee away, casually, as if by
accident. The other hand, the face, the spirit
are kissing and caressing her boy friend.
What a divided person she is!

Three high school age blacks stare at the
pile in barbaric wonder, for black people are
not as civilized as this. 'Right on,' they

murmur, and so do I. A fireman sticks his
head in the rear door. He goes away again.
The lights come up and a long, single, agonized
cry rises from the audience: 'Berkeley. . . .'

A real actress makes you see not only
the people but the whole scene,
clothes, background, expression.
If the room itself doesn't
fit, you don't feel right. So we don't use
settings anymore.
For a contemporary play
we like to arrange bare planks, piled
in intersecting platforms,

and we depend on you to imagine water
flowing down
over them.
And now the young are almost all able
to live there all day.

Suddenly a pool of light appears in the middle
of the plant. We worked all night
in the offices upstairs. The contract depended
on it. At five o'clock
in the morning, we staggered down to the plant
floor and started one of the lathes.
Then we lost track. By
light though we were over the hump
and when the navy inspector
arrived we had most of the line set up
and with the help of the girls in the cafeteria,
who held up the early
coffee, by the time the inspector took up his

position, we were ready.

Squeezing by you in a narrow kitchen
my hand, as if by accident
brushes your hip. My body rubs delicately
against yours. My other hand
touches your hip, going away.

We always know when it has happened
to us, but we never
know when it has happened to other people.

The Huey Newton Trial

September, Oakland. I know perfectly well what the past
really contains, and it's not like the events I remember, like the
Supreme Court decision of 1954 against school segregation. That
decision is a fact, but it's not anybody's personal history. The
history is my memory of the civics teacher who slipped one day
and called me a nigger.

I move on, I'm in Selma, Alabama, for the triumphant march
to Montgomery, trying to ward off the memory of America in the
'40s and '50s by engaging in the fight for black civil rights. In
those years travelling with my family was preceded by getting
a list of 'good' hotels from the Urban League. I would leaf
through the list: three hotels in Utah, we'll have to drive straight
through from Denver . . . No, no, there's no way to get satisfaction
for those years by going to Selma.

Nor can I afford to remember how many times I've been in a
strange, white neighborhood bar and suddenly heard a glass
smash to the floor behind me. 'Nigger,' murmur the pittsburgh
Irishmen, 'get out of here before we skin your black ass!'

I broke my beer bottle on the table, held the jagged end
before me like a dagger, backed toward the door and *got out!*

And as though the deep past weren't enough trouble, the
way a black man looks at this country, and responds to it, has
changed two or three times in the last five years—each time
darker and more violent. But I can also feel that in these days
of bewildering change a black man can hardly survive without
a new sensibility—one that exposes before it heals. So alto-
gether, I shouldn't be surprised at the violence of the emo-
tion that seizes me, arriving at the Alameda County Courthouse for the Huey Newton trial. But I am.

The proportions of the courthouse are all wrong. The building
has a short-legged look, not at all like the graceful county court-

house of my pennsylvania youth. I see a political ugliness here, as well as an architectural one; behind every door stand a couple sheriff's deputies, dressed in grey, fully armed, with Mace, and with at least one walkie-talkie. The residential hills of the city are on the other side of nearby Lake Merritt. The view across the lake should be that of a Mediterranean scene—the morning mist, the terraced aspect of the hills, the white buildings —but I still see Oakland, California, where the police department recruits in the deep South for officers.

There's never been a really hot riot here, but ever since the organization of the Black Panther Party almost two years ago, party members have been skirmishing with Oakland police— from mass media name-calling to pig-watching patrols to political organizing attempts to gun battles. And suddenly young blacks in the Oakland ghetto are wearing the characteristic black leather jacket of the Panthers, and similar organizations appear in other cities across the country. Now the founder of the party, Huey P. Newton, is accused of murder of an Oakland cop and assault on another.

On the twelfth street side of the courthouse, spectators are already gathering: black children not yet in their teens, a young white couple, several political activists from Berkeley, a middle-aged black dancer. The scene changes. It's ten in the morning and I'm in a room outside court, leaning forward, hands on a rack. The deputy sheriff frisks me, humming a song from a musical comedy of the '50s: it might as well be spring. His glare is a hot spot on my back because I've given him some shit by asking if he enjoys his work. Bending, he feels my balls for explosive materials, and straightens. Finishes his search for hidden weapons by running his hand in a contemptuous swipe straight down my back, saying 'Thank you.'

As though I had just gone through a decompression chamber, I pass into the courtroom, the same old American place. The sounds of the world are cut off. Lowell Jensen, assistant district attorney, presents a series of witnesses, ending with a criminalist, John Davis, a small man with a blond handlebar moustache, who works for the Oakland force. Even Charles Garry, chief defense counsel, respects Davis, who talks about a ballistics test the way black men are supposed to talk about fried chicken—headlong, American, unquestionable.

Davis sits in the witness chair, but he has a little button

in his hand, a little remote control button, which makes slides
flash on a screen. The jury stares at a slide of a section of a slug.
They don't precisely understand the significance of it, but they're
impressed anyway. The room is only half-lit. A newsman darts out.
'Bailiff, no one is to enter or leave this room while the lights are
off,' bellows Superior Court Judge Monroe Friedman. He sits,
old, dispassionate, behind the bench, remembering the scenes
of his youth—the very area where the shooting took place—
where he used to deliver newspapers, sixty years ago. He doesn't
like to hear west Oakland described by defense witnesses as a
ghetto, and he frowns. What, not part of the American main-
stream? You tell me, Friedman says, if anywhere in Alameda
County black people aren't allowed to register or vote. Garry
stares at him, speechless, and the judge sinks back into his large
chair, vindicated.

He appears to doze from time to time when testimony is
boring, starting alert again at a change in rhythm of a voice, a
rise of pitch or a pause. One afternoon he abruptly adjourns court
and, black robe flying, plunges from the bench and pops out his
little chamber door in search of the judicial urinal.

The courtroom is thus full of white man's law, feeling and
sensibility. There was a conspiracy on the part of the entire
Oakland establishment to get Huey, Garry states flatly in his
opening statement, but several female jurors frown outright
at his accusation.

I'm shifting in my seat, I'm wishing this struggle were between equal forces, and that Huey and the other Panthers were
emissaries of unseen black regiments, cities and presences—and
therefore safe, according to a kind of ghetto diplomacy, like the
gunboat diplomacy of the British. Trouble with one of our cit-
izens? Touch him and next week a gunboat floats in the harbor,
guns pointing at the town.

Herbert Heanes, the surviving cop, walks into the courtroom,
cat-like, tender. Instantly I have the picture of a frontier marshall,
tall, lonely and handsome until a bullet comes from the dark and
smashes into his arm. He takes two more bullets; he's knocked
to his knees, his eyes swiveling frantically toward the bulk of
the post office construction project to the left.

A few seconds later he's sprawled on the seat of a police
car, radioing hysterically for help, 'Nine 40 B, 940 B, officer

needs assistance at Seventh and Willow.' His voice is now
dead and vibrationless. He has a duodenal ulcer and colitis,
an emotional disorder; he sleeps with a loaded pistol under
his pillow; he looks drugged as he testifies now. He never ac-
tually saw Huey with a gun, but he was walking behind him and
the dead cop when Huey spun around and began to struggle with
the cop, John Frey. Heanes felt the shot in his right arm and heard
a storm of shots. Listening to him, I realize what depression is.
Sometimes it's the heaviness of the smashing blow against the
bone of the arm, sometimes it's the heaviness you carry around
with you all the time. Already I feel myself at work arranging
the material of the case—events themselves, my response to
them, the deeper political significance—so it will be a suitable
part of my past, much as Heanes has arranged his own to pre-
pare a nest for himself against the shock of the bullet.

The black people in the room seem frozen with similar
rage and despair, the bailiffs look bored. We require recess
as relief from tension, like a headache pill. Reporters talk shop,
Huey's family chat. An occasional laugh rings out. It's sunny.
Then recess is over, court is again in session, tension returns.
There is an emotional meaning to this trial more threatening—
and more important—than even its political implications but I
can't hold it, my mind slips from its cogs, I'm no longer on the
verge of an astounding revelation and the trial gets underway
again.

'Dear Miss Tucker, you don't know me but a friend gave me
your address . . .' No, the black soldier doesn't want you to put
the letter in your own words, he just wants you to put the syntax
and the spelling straight so he can copy it; because even if black
men have high school diplomas that doesn't mean they can read
or write. You're damn right this trial is political, says Huey, nervous, complaining of the cold. The judge, very alert in such matters, motions the bailiff to the thermostat to adjust it. At recess
Huey stands, flapping his arms up and down, as if warming up
for some athletic contest, as Garry teases him.

Fifty or sixty times, Huey's been stopped by the pigs of the
Oakland police force, he tells us, and on the morning of October 28,
1967, as he and a friend, Gene McKinney, drive down Willow
Street, I wonder if he thought anything special was about to
happen? The red police light is flashing and white officer

John Frey comes up to the car.

'Well, well. Who do we have here. The great, great Huey P. Newton?' he says.

The truth of this is so strong that I sense the setting: the dark, the mist, the construction project to the south, the all-night restaurants to the north, and the red light blinking.

Heanes pulls up to cover. Frey frisks Huey and orders him to the rear, walking slightly behind him. Frey silently, wordlessly, halts Huey. Why? Huey half-wheels, opens his law book.

'You can take that law book and shove it up your ass!' Frey straightarms Newton, who falls to one knee. Frey's big service revolver comes up. A flower of fire, Huey's belly feels like someone poured hot soup on it. He hears a thunder of shots. Instantly everything is whirling, he is helped into a car, the car is travelling.

Outside Kaiser Hospital, the ramp to the emergency treatment room seems impossibly high, but Huey, shot in the abdomen, crawls over it and lurches into the emergency room. Corrine Leonard, nurse in charge, demands to see his Kaiser Health Plan card. Soon, the police come dashing in, leap on him and handcuff his hands over his head, stretching his stomach wound painfully. The doctor on duty strolls in. Huey is raving about black power. 'Shut up,' the doctor yells. He slams an injection of Thorazine into the wounded man.

The bus companies can treat you like a dog if you're late on your run, at least in the San Francisco-Oakland Bay Area, and Henry Grier, the star prosecution witness, sharply insists that he's always on time. (But Tommy Miller was just talking to another man about how late the bus was, when the #82 Oakland to Hayward bus pulled up, Grier driving, and then travelled down Seventh to Willow.)

During jury selection the defense attorney has repeatedly warned the jury not to expect any Perry Mason foolishness at this trial—'You don't expect me to produce the actual murderer, do you?' Garry said, but of course Grier hasn't heard him, and is unaware of the irony running through his testimony.

It takes a lot of energy to be something, but it takes even more to be nothing, in the long run. Grier has this kind of brief, costly force available to him, and it, along with his dramatic behavior, the racially disloyal character of his testimony, his background, and his funny insistence about his punctuality, induces in me a disbelief of his description so strong I can hardly keep from shouting.

God knows how many times he's practiced this story. All those years in the navy, for example. He calls Garry 'counciller' and he leaps from the witness chair to a chart to show where the bus was. The bus is coasting to a stop, he turns to the judge to explain, and he sees Huey and a cop walking toward the last police 'vehicle,' another cop walking behind them, when suddenly Newton spins, reaches in his shirt, pulls a gun and opens up.

Grier tries to call the dispatcher: an officer is being shot before his very eyes. He's terribly upset. He's playing a scene before millions of people. He thinks he's on television. And he walks down from the chair and lays his hand on Huey in identification.

Huey stares at Grier in loathing, because in a statement given to the police only an hour and a half after the shooting, Grier told an entirely different story. In that statement Grier said Frey's assailant was a peewee sort of a guy in a tan jacket, black shirt, and a hat. Now, on the witness stand, Grier denies the statement.

Recess. Grier, standing down from the stand and surrounded by the county investigators and bailiffs, lights a cigarette. The only black man on that side of the room, he smokes and stares at the ceiling. Sometimes it occurs to me that none of us is any different, really, from him; but no, if I were in his place, my heart would be rotting away.

Last year, shortly before the shooting, John Frey gave a talk at Clayton Valley high school, out in the suburbs, and he was pretty contemptuous in it, using the word 'nigger' at least once. There was a little scandal about it in Alameda County at the time, but the incident assumes much more importance now, since it goes to indicate that Frey was a racist cop. Against his will, Thomas Parsons, 18, a member of the class that heard Frey's talk, appears on the stand. We learn that Parsons' neighbors in Concord, California, threatened to burn him out if he testified for the defense, but Parsons himself lies about the incident, according to the sworn testimony of Faye Stender, assistant defense counsel. His behavior is typical of that of almost all the prosecution witnesses, and even the establishment reporters mostly concede that the feel of the case is wrong, and certainly the presence alone of Huey's passenger in the car should introduce the element of reasonable doubt. Nevertheless, nobody knows what the jury will do. Certainly they are sensitive to some of the other pressures involved in the trial—such as the possible reaction from the white community if Newton is freed, and the probable reaction from the black community if he isn't.

A black announcer for a local radio station sits in the hall by the sixth-floor pressroom, his head down, waiting for the verdict. A stack of notebooks is piled in a corner. He picks one up, leafs through it, staring at the shorthand symbols, and flips it away. Huey's family sit together in another corner of the hall, along with Laverne Williams, Huey's beautiful, long-legged girl, we are all desperately waiting. What is Harper, the black foreman of the jury, doing? Is he holding the line for acquittal? Who are these black lawyers in their white on white shirts? What about Huey's brothers Walter and Lee, sawing at the air, always trying to say it?

Sunday night. The verdict is in: Voluntary manslaughter. Two to 15 years. On the sixth floor again, Doris, Huey's sister immediately collapses when she hears the verdict. Laverne Williams supports her as the photographers crowd around for pictures. 'Be human, be human,' Laverne pleads brokenly to the photographers, but television is too hungry for life. The photographers pursue the family toward the elevator, they rake the interior of it with light until the operator, a fat, hostile white man in a Hawaiian shirt, closes the door. In the basement of the building reserve units of the California Highway Patrol and the sheriff's department are stationed, in case of trouble from the black residents of Oakland, and rumor has it that 8,000 National Guardsmen are waiting in additional reserve at Camp Parks, a Job Corps center about 30 miles away.

On the sixth floor of the courthouse again, another elevator door opens, and defense attorney Garry gets out, looking like pale hell. He is very disappointed with the verdict, he says, it makes no sense from a legal or evidentiary point of view. He implies that it makes no difference if you consider the verdict to be a half-triumph, in that it represented a response by the jury to pressure by black people. Justice was still not served.

Suddenly, beyond all power to prevent it, the trial recedes from me. Upstairs, Huey Newton must be bursting with intolerable energy, but outside the courthouse the streets are as empty on Sunday night as if nothing had happened. A young girl reporter for an underground newspaper cries quietly, not knowing whether her side has won a victory or not.

A dusty Volkswagen with a peace sticker on the bumper pulls up to the curb and a thin woman with long blonde hair leans out, speaking softly. I can't hear her. She whispers again, is the verdict in yet? What does a manslaughter conviction mean? Will there be a demonstration? I don't know, I don't know, I'm already diffusing into the night.

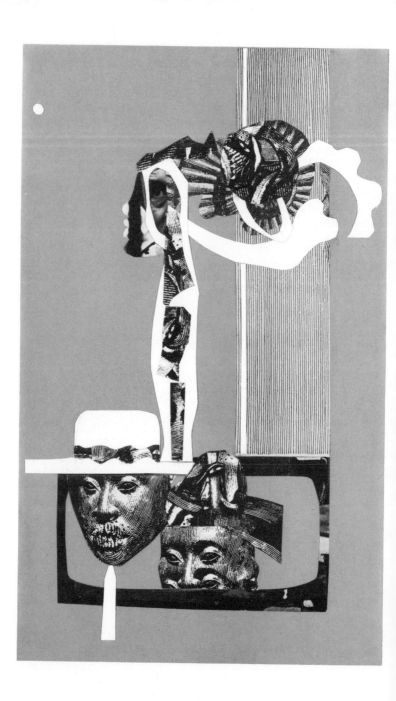

David
Henderson

Felix of the Silent Forest

to Felix the Cat /Noveltytoons, USA & Ed Krasnow

Felix   you horizon dancer
Who are these people who say
they have known you a long time?
who are those friends
who attack you by the same handle?

In this age of debarkment
        epoch of mass inter-regimentation
    no longer have we cause to stay away
for not diving in
        it is the age of epaulet & picket line
        vertigo and alliance

Felix walks here and there
Felix walks the City
sometimes fast sometimes slow
like a dying man wanting everything he sees
not wanting to desist   to leave
never to allow Fate Palance
to have his way

Felix stops & then goes on

Often
Felix walks the City hungry in every sense
of every gastric salivating phenomenon
thighs   to eyes   to mouth
        He is wooed by Tad's $1.19 steaks
as well as 2 for 25¢ Hamburgers on forty-second street
        the Crossroads—

He has bent in supplication
over 25¢ potato & gravy meals
in Pole Town Avenue "A"
as often as fried chicken fantasies
down Avenue "D"—the downtown Harlem
        On upper Seventh Avenue
he watches his plate being piled high
with fish & fried potatoes
the oil soaks and drips down
Felix thinks of cholestorol   chest pains   heart spasms
            yet   he passes fish
        to watered-down hot sauce   to mouth with gladness
plus joy to the plastic-blotter bread
which picks up the grease

Felix
sits in Martin's Bar   Smiths   Blarney Stones
Bowery deformed men's bars   the Silver Rail Harlem
Shalomar-by-Randolph's   Regan's on Staten Island
the Jerome Avenue Spa or Sylvia's Blue Morocco Bronx NY
        Felix sits in any bar 3 or 4 for a dollar
wondering if
anyone he loves
wonders where he is

Boston Road Blues

I

Boston Road is as wide as a boulevard
but lacks the classic grandeur of verdure
Tenements and bleacher-like stoops
line the cobblestone expanse through Mid-Bronx
the cars & trucks sound faster   then they go
often
        cobbled stone runs up into pink brick
of the Housing Authority's stadium

ride a speeding Bonneville
along this main street
and you will see the Negroes waiting on either side
on stoops on dinette and aluminum beach chairs
like the retired
                    bop cap and sneakered Jews
of the Grand Concourse

at 149th st Boston Road passes perpendicular
under the El
then the Shadow Box Cabaret, Freddy's, the Oasis,
Sylvia's Blue Morocco, Paradise Club, Goodson's
on to Crotona Park
where one summer of the fifth decade
the burning Enchanters bopped down
on the Crowns, the Bathgate Avenue Stompers,
and the Scorpions from PR
in rapid fury & succession
and now   where the same adolescents
play softball for the Youth Board.

and the inlet to Public School 55
the swinging "Cadillacs" always took
Earl at the fishtail wheel
responding to 'hey Speedo' when in reality
his real name *was* Mister Earl
singing as he was
                    his teeth jumbled & contorted
the Cadillacs personnel tall and short
sundry and aloof
gleaming bemused hair
the only top to the convertible
the only road map to the sun.
packed in front of all-girl Jane Addams
their marijuana their argot their ornate auto
routed by a militant lady principal . . .
All the quartets sang louder
when the Cadillacs cruised Brook Avenue—

P.S. 55 is to be integrated this autumn
the Cadillacs have passed (Earl now with the Coasters)
and the Housing Authority has arrived
as influential as Jesus
as gigantic as the Tennessee Valley Authority.
1501 Boston Road is Bronx C.O.R.E.
    (stompers have risen to politics)
Herb Callender   Isiah Brunson   knife riding
    shit talking   genius pacifist—
The road swirls until ghetto limits
where   above two hundred street
        it becomes tar smooth   single similar double
caucasian family homes
and Boston Road becomes Boston Post Road.

II

When I was a singer
I stayed on Boston Road
among the cabarets & the singers: the Dells,
the Mellotones, the Cadillacs . . .
    our quartet calling ourselves Starsteppers
    (perhaps to insure a goal
                    other than a ghetto)
evinced no concept of space save
                    where the cobblestone Road
and the bleachers-on-residence tampered to a point
where The Road became post—itself.

by twilight the clubs released their exotic lures
Sylvia's Blue Morocco sheds blue light both neon & real
on sidewalk and cobblestones between Shabazz Beauty Parlor
& Denzil's Fabulous candystore
Velvet Blue drapes hang ceiling to floor
and all to be seen inside is the spotlighted face
of the singer the dim blue faces of the music
the soloist the master of ceremonies —heads
                  truncated in blackness
puppeted by galloping   Hessians from Scarsdale
And Freddy's white enamel front white lights
all outward   upward
harlem jazz exude bandstand tall   /mixing
        with moth & mosquito insect-serendipity

all white light reflected spill over bleacher sitters
parked car residers, vigillers, standee's dispersed
                    and reassembled.
The tenements soar skyward
half white light half black dwindling to sky
stars dismissed by energy of mortals.
        & for a moment Club 845 the combo in the window (display)
sunday combination cocktail sips jam sessions
for bored number players 4 pm to 8 pm
after church and before chicken.

III
We Starsteppers
                    wore the same type cord suit blue
and as a rhythm 'n' blues singer my PAT BOONE endorsed
one afforded uniform discomfort as just reward
for being in a hurry in an 125th Street clothing store
    (probably thinking the street was in Harlem)
and contributing to the corny man (:Patrick Alphonse Boone
                                Columbia University 1959)
who stole Little Richard's tunes
& parodied them into a fortune.
Little Richard receiving lyricist royalties
but no TV show
no life insurance & old age compensation
only a backwater church Southern
the God
the Holy Ghost
the Son
                of a pagan country.

The Starstepper organization carried four singers
three managers and a lopsided Cadillac
                Let's take a cocktail sip
    and talk of the crippled '55 Caddy in 1960
                —the epoch of reform—
Buddy, our main manager, wrote and recorded a song
called "SCHBOOM"
then the Crewcuts swept away the bread
the Man couldn't use a colored group on TV 1954
Buddy got the writer's royalties   /tho
and I would suppose that Sunset Boulevard

in a brand new white caddy convertible
things travel quickly
as that colored group did in L.A.
singing the Crewcuts song.
                          Spenser—yet another manager—
torpedo-head lank lipped   sold ''Let the Little Girl Dance''
                          for one hundred bills
Fat Billy Bland & three young colored girls took over
and Spenser
because he had a hit record (moneywise not his)
sported his long red conk all over Tin Pan Alley
haranguing the Brill Building   and shit
borrowing the singled axled Cadillac
by day
to return at night
hair out of gas   car out of gas
spent

IV
So
after record hops (anywhere and everyone)
community center and house party gigs
background harmony (of our own invention) for
BIG TIME RECORD COMPANY
ten dollars a day
steady gigging Goodson's (gay) Little Club
on Boston-Road-by-Randolph
                    (The clientele loved fresh young talent
            they said / Goodson too)
We recorded Broadway in a white Cadillac
High School boys & old hustlers
Handkerchiefs Sabu over Pozner-fresh conk
black and red

Then one day I told Goodson, sir
the Starsteppers have a recording out now
and we are not accepting anymore   clubdates
on Boston Road, our managers have instructed me
to tell you.
              ZAP!

Outside the "Little" club on the Road that last night
I watched the tiny attracter light
swing its eerie strobic beam twenty times yellow
a minute
            to the street stones of steep 167th
long across Boston Road   the island in front of A&P
through the trees   catching the tenements high
then diffused and broken runs   to re/wing
the tiny canopy of Goodson's Little Club
                then down 167th again
   (which in the Bronx has a common level of understanding)
take Sunset Boulevard
                        to give a sense of dimension

Later
the higher forms of publicity
our managers had subsequently informed
Mr. Goodson of
consisted of giving all available copies
of our hit record to friends
occasional pilgrimages downtown
for pep talks about word-of-mouth
waiting days   waiting nights
New York Radio stations   New Jersey Stations
            (WVNJ played it at six one morning)
            JOCKO MURRAY THE K ALLEN FREED CLAY COLE
            DR JIVE BRUCE THE MOOSE announcing to their
   boys & girls the new boss hit by the starsteppers
"You're Gone"   the flip side that you'll wig over
"The First Sign of Love"

We were told
it often takes months   up to a year
for a record to be picked up on
sometimes they start big on the Coast
we waited
six months   a year
reading CASHBOX weekly
we waited (never to Goodson again)
we waited
and after a while
started singing to ourselves once more.

Bopping

My main men and I bopped
to general agreement (like the toast to 'the boys upstate'
                  before every bottle of Paradise or
                  Thunderbird wine)
down cats
we bopped to give cause to the causes
that died before they got to us.

I remember the arm pumping cap crowned blades
of my boyhood
their elemental gait talking
deep beneath my eyes . . .
the list at waist and trunk
   whip of an arm
& abrupt   then long wing-tipped stride
of days when we had to show ourselves love
in difficult pretensions
           as if speaking words of self-love
      was too remote   a performance
   when   before the fact
we understood all too well
the action of the thrust.

We maneuvered
to turn that way in dawns or dusk
of the eternal wars
among ourselves   our gangs:
           the Crowns Chaplins Sportsmen
Boston Baldies Young Sinners Enchanters Duschon Lords—
because talking   after all   is too little of glamour
to the hungry   the ugly   the mean

We bopped when about to fight
and we bopped when happy
all in our own slight variances
known to the members of the Road
and known to the similar bops
of the roaming hordes

From Avenue "D"   to Red Hook
thru March Projects   then Crown Heights
Prospect Avenue in the Bronx & also in Brooklyn
The Fifth Avenue Armory on 141st & the Harlem River
Bronx River Housing   forty-three   fifty-five
99 center Boston Road
From Winters to graduation
From street duels
until
wedlock   or the cops
shot us down
bopping . . .

Fork of the West River (5)

from my windows
i hear the rain of the water hydrants
seems like water brings the breezes
seems like night time brings the breezes

by summer-in-the city days
i walk huge dust storms
along the popular avenues
looking for my son

sometimes i walk uptown
facing the palisades from across the great hudson
where the cathedrals of higher education loom high
against the sky

sometimes i walk thru central park
and find
that as we near the ghetto
the park becomes a mountain
which we must overcome
for a good fish sandwich

So We Went to Harlem

So we went to Harlem.
The many-fabled letter-men—two black, one white—
Went to Harlem to screw broads.

Roaring through the streets
—me driving—
Hood flying off on Park Avenue
—me choking with laughter.
Cal blasting Spanish at Puerto Ricans
Coming from dance. One sauntering over,
Cal mitigating, ¿*Que pasa?* man.
¿*Que pasa?* sweetly flowing.

Three thorns
Precipitous
For the drain
Coming from a Brooklyn Beatnik party
Drunk
                        happy
        and full of sap
                        —*going to, Harlem!*

David at the wheel high driving like a speed-gone fool
Flawing greatly guffawing . . . gently leaking
Richard laughing in spasms Cal cajoling before arriving
And me passing the wine in that rollicking Plymouth
So light
So gay
On the verge of flight but not over
That Ghetto
                Going' to see your baby?
                Naw! goin' to HARLEM—get some broads!

II
So we cantered into Harlem rambling the car apark
On some glittering street . . .
HARLEM! the exotic land of the Midnight Air
And nefarious mediocrity. HARLEM! where brown men
And women dance all day and sing all night.
HARLEM! Where I was spawned

             Where Richard was labeled
             Where Calvin is to gasp to his death.

So we arrived in Harlem:
Up and down   125th Street
                   126th Street
                   127th Street
                   128th, 129th   . . . *up and down*
—*Lookin' for a good time boys?*
                                 up and down
—*Eight dollahs all you need. Any broad you want!*
                                 up and down
—*What's happenin' fellas?*
                                 up and down
—*Hey!*
             (I ask white Richard if he likes any
             special one. He doesn't know.)
                                 up and down
—*What's your name sweetheart.*
                                 up and down
             BABY! HONEY! SWEETHEART! LOVER!
up
             BROADS—ASSES—BUTTER—BROWN—HEAVEN!
             the sweeter the berry—
                                 down
Across and below   . . . *across and below*

Woman (a black hostess) approaches eyes on Richard
She asks if he would like to come with her. Richard
un-articulate looks to me—Gunga Din
Cal's off somewhere
Richard doesn't speak
Silence implies negation
Business law?
             (but of course may imply
             affirmation—depending on
             the circumstances)
Could silence under obligation to speak imply guilt?
   Woman leaves at my power of attorney
     Richard ruminates
       Cal returns

Richard decides he wants her
I obtain—David the Pimping Rinehart—no
Commission . . . Please!
Richard meets broad formally, is enchanted and strolls
Away with atavistic visions of Ghetto copulation.
Calvin and I joy for strange dissimilar reasons.

Long time later when Richard should have reached that
Fulsome orgasm we find him still walking the streets,
Having not yet commemorated but still happy-faced.
          The Woman:
Round semblance of fine shit-talking and Oblique to
the sap that coagulates at the Poetress never to flow—
          Richard:
White strange goofy deep-in-love: giggling cuddle kiss
Smile   high   —too deep . . . will never
                  lose love to a Ghetto

III

So in going to Harlem and being meandered throughout
We: the chick, Richard, Cal and I
                 Getting Black
Market wine. Cal talking nigger-shit, Richard jealous
Of his tax-free purchase. Cal cajoling at last
To the final reluctance. Me sopping wine and dripping,
Knowing Richard's fate.   Not knowing if I felt exultation
Pain or guilt submitting generously to the wine—

IV

So we left Harlem
After Richard had been taken at last to some hotel
And told by the broad to wait outside while she
"arranged things" and Richard waiting and trusting
      And waiting . . .

Cal and I finally found Richard wandering about
The same block lost and looking. Richard having
Given the Hustler all of his money and ours, to
The Ghetto he trusted and winding up lost.
Richard being lost for one hour and saying in the car
On the way back to the Village that he still liked her.

Richard
Lost once in a Ghetto
So he who went to Harlem will never lose love to a Ghetto
Richard
Who loved one night a Ghetto
Richard
Who sat in the speeding car very much confused
And didn't help retrieve the hood when it flew off again
Cal thinking
And David
Driving too hard to think . . .

Patricia Parker

From the Cavities of Bones

This at last is bone of my bones and flesh of my flesh; she shall be called Woman, because she was taken out of Man.
——Genesis I : 23

from cavities of bones
  spun
      from caverns of air
i, woman—bred of man
taken from the womb of sleep;
i, woman that comes
before the first.

to think second
to believe first
  a mistaken conundrum
    erased by the motion of years.
i, woman, i
  can no longer claim
  a mother of flesh
  a father of marrow
I, Woman, must be
  the child of myself.

I Followed a Path

Do not go gentle into that good night
——Dylan Thomas

I followed a path.
    the path—it led
to somewhere. Curved
around space leading
me from my youth.
I met an old man.
"Old man, give back
my youth."
He gave me a
gold pitcher
with a hole in it.

I followed a path.
    the path—it led
to marbles & jacks
& dolls, mother,
house, school, love.
I met a little girl.
"Little girl, give back
my youth."
She ran away.
Her mother had told her not to speak
to strangers.

I followed a path.
    the path—it led
to a mirror.
I saw a face - not mine.
A face with lines
leading to pain & joy,
song and dances.
I wanted to dance again.
I skipped over guilt;
I laughed at failure.
For one moment,
I chased the lines away.

The lines crept back.
"Mirror, give back
my youth."
The face in the mirror
turned away.

I followed a path.
    the path—it led
to a river.
I bathed myself.
"River, give back
my youth."
The river was muddy.

I followed a path.
    the path—it led
to an unowned grave.
It did not say me,
  But it was mine.

Assassination

It's Hunt's catsup
splattered over the country
like in some movie
and the dead guy
shifted ever so slightly
when a rock fell too close
    but it is real—

this dead man
twitches in our minds
and
we stop to scratch.

A Family Tree

Cursed by Canaan; a slave of slaves shall he be to his brothers.
——Genesis 9 : 25

Pitch sun-child drowns in the Mississippi,
washes away chains of loneliness, floats
a drum beat on the Nile.

Daughter of Ham lies on a church floor;
filled in orgasm with her Maker,
a spent lover ignorant of a hard bed.

The sperm of a million nights
sings loud over the southern skies.
—Sirens to a nation's conscience.

A babe of illusion has been born.
She will tell the world of rainbows;
And kiss the holes in its eyes.

Sometimes My Husband

Sometimes my husband
acts
just like a man . . .

dishes are evil / you know
they can destroy the spirit . . .

Washing dishes should
be outlawed

paper plate nirvana!

long live dixie cups!

> . . . tomorrow i am going to lose
> my temper—
>
> i will destroy all the dishes
> that i missed last week—

Adam David Miller

The Hungry Black Child

lord
forgive me
if i twist the sunset
but when evening twist my belly
i see red
walking the field the woods
the houses on my street
white
burning burning

Crack in the Wall Holds Flowers

After each Quake
New cracks appear in the wall;
These fissures forced by cataclysm
Hold flowers.

This vast natural damage
Presaged always by rumblings
Deep in things maternal breeds lilacs
That hang in a nook near the edge of the sun.

My uneasiness
Reminded by a niche now brown,
Is not soothed by the prospect of flowers.

The Africa Thing

What is Africa to thee?

Let's shuffle

Paint that horn
on backwards—
Knock me some skin   Blow! O

They say home
is a place
in the mind
where you
can rest
when you're tired
not where
your great great
great grandfather
had his farm

Africa?

Africa   beble be
is that old man   ba
in the pickin field   bo
making that strange high sound   bibob
and all the people following   blaaba
Africa is a sound   ba ba
Africa   buddi di oooooo
is the touch   rock a dioooo
of that old woman
your mother could not stand   do oo do o
but did respect
who caught you as you fell
and held you
and rocked you

Fat black bucks in a wine barrel   boom
boom
What is Africa to thee   bam
thou thoo thum   boom
I smell the sweat of an english scum   boom boom

—Mamma, Mamma, but he *does*
It's *not* just his breath
He stink
Hushsssh, chile
Somebody'll hear you
Say *smell.*

Africa
is the look
of Tweebie Mae
Snapping her
head around
before she took off
   Caint ketch me
in the soft dark
You caught her

Africa
is all them roots
and conjurs
and spells
wails and chants
(say blues and hollers)
and all them stories
about Stackalee
and John Henry
and Bodidly
and the camp meetings
where the wrestling
and head and head
the foot races
the jumping
the throwing

We brought all that down

to dance at birth
when you're sick
take a wife
lose your luck
when you die

and singing in the woods
    in the fields
  when you walk
and singing on the levies
    on the chain gang
    in the jail
singing and dancing when you pray
and dancing by the light of the moon
until you drop.

Africa is the singing
of these lines
of me
of you
of love
singing.

Clarence Major

This Temple

                was he 17 years a
boy started the dove
                in mind mind, air mail or
the wings, just pigeons, a flight of
                them scattering peanutshells on Drexel
in front of the Park Theatre, the sky of my
                homeland. My arms at my sides, I
will never be this old man feeding these birds.
                Scattering trash, that scattering
the sound, the color it creates in the exact
                time it takes to frighten them always
caught my eye. But I knew that I wrote
                of doves precisely for Ron P. & his
White Dove, which had nothing to do with
                THIS BLACK RECEPTACLE
"a castle of lust
                & I even (quote me not beyond this
point: I even said it was a search comparable
                like a crucifixion) NAILS DRIVEN INTO
THIS TEMPLE TO HOLD THE CAREFREE BLOOD STILL while
                warm, to cage, to destroy any paradox.
But it was all about love, even Drexel parkway
                in front of the Park Theatre—
those pigeons, not doves

Tud

Found in the blackest
corner
    with a tail making perfect
circles   going thirty eight turns
     per second
a nose as dry
drier even than a
black walnut

                  Sheilo's
imperatives were
detectable in this
    yet nameless puppy
    symbolless black
black terrier-and-something-else puppy with
the blackest happy
eyes

Tud became the second
untouchable superstition in
our mutual life
          (the first being the
eternal probably endlessly probable nature of our
marriage ritual)

            Walking unacclaimedly from
the magnanimous structure, the comprehensive ASPCA
her strut
        dedicated to a joyful language that
snatched passers-by eyeballs and
dimples deep into
cheeks and little ole
ladies stopped to
              run-
              down
        dog psychology to our idiomatic skull fumes
THE WORLD THE NEW ILLUSTRATED WORLD was so
worriedly modern, clear
        they constantly kept coming

to Tud's tender excitement
          WITH THEIR MIDTOWN WHOLEHEARTED WINNING
                SUPPORT AND SMILES
"Tud? Named for Harriet Tubman. Didn't have
          the heart to call her Tub."
                                    She licked their lips
their colloquial cheeks and
in detail danced alphabetical arrangements around
          their abbreviated wool origins with
her illuminated innocent multi-stepped dance
                              on
not only this first crowded venture into our
          country's contained collages of
                slangly and convenient
                    VIOLENCE and relevant and sadistic
                    LOVE but into our
          quivering population, people people
downtown downhome in
Tompkins Square Park where
                              with black racy TuddyDud
nursemaid Sheilo is suddenly consumed
                with a brainstroke of love
for her majesty three decades thick
in profusion
                mentally handcuffed by Tud's valuable
charming squandering energy in
          ! EXPLOSIVE jumps   of brain-
splitting joy

                        while I
am encircled by the situation of Tud's mounting
and astoundingly aggressive bombings
              (operating as barks, growls, yelps)
                          during her
first task of heat
          BOMBING OF THE WATERWAYS OF MY MIND
simply in the house
or even when she turns to pinpoint even
big male dogs
              to do them to subdue them
                  into pacification, humping

uncamouflagedly huge serious strokes
of combat sex strategy
                         into their baffled squeeze
just anywhere natural in parks
even on Sheilo's leg
          on my nominated arms
blindly
          unable to empty our cultured affection for
her we
increase our unsophisticated "slogan of love" ,
               FORTIFICATION AND PROTECTION for this
dumb
          stupor-of-happiness-consumed happy
Spring hairdropping elite mut who wont
eat
    anything less valid than premium steaks who
survives our inscrutable presence and
defies
our stupid stupid
                    radical alternatives to
life
with her wet tactical nose sloppy
mindless lovableactivist tongue

               by
simply fullfilling the simplest requirements
     of communication, and nothing
          nothing more

Longlegs

her Cool was a
northern thing
brought from the south

          she really stretched out in NYC

               long-

legs now step
silently in narrow streets
in the village

sleep on easy floors
dark travels on
high tongue eye trips
or the indispensable

devotion to music she
works for her Cool
        she really stretched out for real

in protective winter
nights her yoga and

diluted footfalls thru
parks of drums, night

challenge the tender pot
reek LSD, even beyond acid

to hieroglyphics on the
flesh of her reference

figures that rigid-
situations put pressure

thru after all europe
mexico west coast & NYC

could even define, or should
necessarily   she just

is a rapid position-girl
change case memory

of self efficient calm
in her private rites

Dismal Moment, passing

      this is has to be here
because I am dis-
consolated.

                Even summer coming
4 years ago, now enlarges the green
accuracy of nature,
      which we won't see till Mexico, any-
way. I think of my mother when I think
of nature, her beliefs. Those lies in space
hanging there to arrange
human minds like suffixes to structures,
like societies. Or meaning like a sheet flapping
on a back porch, people might still
wash things, hang them up to dry. Like children
playing roots or shock on the side-
where we walk, upsidedown looking at jets go

      not easy like me here, in this opaque opening.
And promise to be All Right
tomorrow, yes yes

Flesh Line, the space

      there is a girl
i used to go with, that is
perform   do   enter   uprear   charm
                 she could in 5 min
i married her
we yapped money & problems, she couldn't
      anymore.   Politics

movement between our lines, our legal

      thing.   I (used) lie beside her
eyes   up
      flight of dark wings caught in a narrow dusty
stair-
way, breaking, things that desperate. My health
you know.
          And talk, lines hung weapons between
us. Like I see her now
               but keep thinking of
her as dead.

Glenn Myles

Express Rider

Express rider
And folkagent
Of dark gold

     Juju-footed

Bufflo soldier
With cobwebbs in
The conked palaces

     Of your mind

Which judge will hear
The Toltec-tracks in
Your trail . . . the deep

     Antler/dancing/deer

The up of the first fruit
Falling in the rings of the
Baobab tree screaming in the

     High grass of your sleep

Where brother rabbit rides
On his forked tongue of speed
To grace your blind fortunes

     On the unpainted corner

Express rider
Bufflo soldier
Which judge will hear

     The up of the first fruit

Where brother rabbit rides
Where brother rabbit rides

     The up of the first fruit

A Poem for Jill/68

You turn your head
To look at
      The
Empty white spot beyond
The junkyard
      Of lower views

And you mark with your
      Finger
As if on glass
       This place you
Cannot see
      As you go behind
The fingertips

With closed lips and stroke
On skin this mark from blank
  Places
     In a life
       A life walking at
The back of your eyes
      A white spot as you go/

But touch and don't see
        The matter
        Filling
         Your
      Feel for it
        You who come

To drink at the full circle of
Speech on the tongue
     The petal hiding the thorn
      And

The whooping-cranes in your brow
        Ready
     To fly

When New Green Tales

When
  New
Green tales
Are fresh in
    The mind
They have the
Character
Of
Old age/coming
            As
Youth is green and
  As
    Age is old—and
Green
    Again.

When New
      Green tales
                Are
                Fresh
      In the mind
They have the character
      Of
      Old age/coming
      As youth is green and
As age is old and green
            Again

Percy/68

I got a friend named Percy
Who Booga-loo's down to
A fine finish
    Just like the Coca Cola
    People on the bathroom
    Wall;
He walks a sweating broad home
Every night,
A newspaper Idol of Annie Oakley
Trying to learn how to shoot straight.
    He dances in the temples of the wolf like
A little-biddy nigger doll with big powers
In congress.
    Oh . . . Percy! the people say. Git it! they
    Say. Work it! they say.
    And all the time he say . . .
"Just like Daniel Boone, coming back to
Work these bears."

Ishmael Reed

I Am a Cowboy in the Boat of Ra

The devil must be forced to reveal any such physical evil (potions, charms, fetishes, etc.) still outside the body and these must be burned.
——**Rituale Romanum,** published 1947, endorsed by the coat of arms and introduction letter from Francis Cardinal Spellman

I am a cowboy in the boat of Ra,
sidewinders in the saloons of fools
bit my forehead   like   O
the untrustworthiness of Egyptologists
who do not know their trips. Who was that
dog-faced man? they asked, the day I rode
from town.

School marms with halitosis cannot see
the Nefertiti fake chipped on the run by slick
germans, the hawk behind Sonny Rollins' head or
the ritual beard of his axe; a longhorn winding
its bells thru the Field of Reeds.

I am a cowboy in the boat of Ra. I bedded
down with Isis, Lady of the Boogaloo, dove
down deep in her horny, stuck up her Wells-Far-ago
in daring midday get away. "Start grabbing the
blue," i said from top of my double crown.

I am a cowboy in the boat of Ra. Ezzard Charles
of the Chisholm Trail. Took up the bass but they
blew off my thumb. Alchemist in ringmanship but a
sucker for the right cross.

I am a cowboy in the boat of Ra. Vamoosed from
the temple i bide my time. The price on the wanted
poster was a-going down, outlaw alias copped my stance
and moody greenhorns were making me dance; while my
                                        mouth's
shooting iron got its chambers jammed.

I am a cowboy in the boat of Ra. Boning-up in
the ol West i bide my time. You should see
me pick off these tin cans whippersnappers. I
write the motown long plays for the comeback of
Osiris. Make them up when stars stare at sleeping
steer out here near the campfire. Women arrive
on the backs of goats and throw themselves on
my Bowie.

I am a cowboy in the boat of Ra. Lord of the lash,
the Loup Garou Kid. Half breed son of Pisces and
Aquarius. I hold the souls of men in my pot. I do
the dirty boogie with scorpions. I make the bulls
keep still and was the first swinger to grape the taste.

I am a cowboy in his boat. Pope Joan of the
Ptah Ra. C/mere a minute willya doll?
Be a good girl and
Bring me my Buffalo horn of black powder
Bring me my headdress of black feathers
Bring me my bones of Ju-Ju snake
Go get my eyelids of red paint.
Hand me my shadow

I'm going into town after Set

I am a cowboy in the boat of Ra

look out Set   here i come Set
to get Set   to sunset Set
to unseat Set   to Set down Set

                    usurper of the Royal couch
                    imposter RAdio of Moses' bush
                    party pooper O hater of dance
                    vampire outlaw of the milky way

Badman of the Guest Professor

for joe overstreet, david henderson, albert ayler
& d mysterious "H" who cut up d rembrandts

1

you worry me whoever you are
i know you didnt want me to
come here but here i am just
d same ; hi-jacking yr stagecoach ,
hauling in yr pocket watches & mak
ing you hoof it all d way to
town . black bart , a robber w/ an
art ; i left some curses in d cash
box so youll know its me

listen man , i cant help it if
yr thing is over , kaputs ,
                finis
no matter how you slice it dick
you are done . a dead duck all out
of quacks ; d nagging hiccup dat
goes on & on w/ out a simple glass
                of water for relief

2

youve been teaching shakespeare for
20 years only to find d joke
                on you
d eavesdropping rascal who got it
in d shins because he didnt know
enough to keep his feet behind d cur
tains ; a sad-sacked head served on a
platter in titus andronicus or falstaff
                too fat to make a go of it
                anymore

3

its not my fault dat yr tradition
was knocked off wop style & left in
d alley w/ pricks in its mouth . i
read abt it in d papers but it was no
        skin off my nose
wasnt me who opened d gates & allowed
d rustlers to slip thru unnoticed . you
ought to do something abt yr security or
        mend yr fences partner
dont look at me if all dese niggers
are ripping it up like deadwood dick ;
doing art d way its never been done . mak
ing wurlitzer sorry he made d piano dat
will drive wolfgang mozart to d tennis
        courts
making smith-corona feel like d red
faced university dat has just delivered china
        some 50 e-leben h bomb experts

i didnt deliver d blow dat drove d
abstract expressionists to mi ladies
linoleum where dey sleep beneath tons of
wax & dogshit & d muddy feet of children or
because some badassed blackpainter done sent
french impressionism to d walls of highrise
        lobbies where dey belong is not my fault

martha graham will never do d jerk
shes a sweet ol soul but her hips
cant roll ; as stiff as d greek
statues she loves so much

4

dese are d reasons you did me nasty
j alfred prufrock , d trick you pull
ed in d bookstore today ; stand in d
corner no peaches for a week , you lemon
you must blame me because yr wife is
ugly . 86-d by a thousand discriminating
saunas . dats why you did dat sneaky thing
i wont tell d townsfolk because you hv
to live here and im just passing thru

5
you got one thing right tho . i did say
dat everytime i read william faulkner i
go to sleep . when i read hemingway i
wish dat one of dem bulls wd hv jumped d
fence & gored his fingers so dat he wdnt hv
taken up so much   good space

fitzgerald wdnt hv known a gangster if one
had snatched zelda & made her a moll tho
        she wd hv been grateful i bet

bonnie of clyde wrote *d saga of suicide
sal* just as d feds were closing in . it is
worth more than d collected works of ts
eliot a trembling anglican whose address
is now d hell dat thrilled him so
last word from down there he was open
ing a publishing co dat will bore d
devil back to paradise

6
& by d way did you hear abt grammar ?
cut to ribbons in a photo finish by
stevie wonder , a blindboy who dances
on a heel . he just came out of d slang
& broke it down before millions .
        it was bloody murder

7
to make a long poem shorter - 3 things
        moleheaded lame w/ 4 or 5 eyes

1) yr world is riding off into d sunset
2) d chips are down & nobody will chance yr i.o.us
3) d last wish was a fluke so now you hv to re
   turn to being a fish
p.s. d enchantment has worn off

dats why you didnt like my reading list right ?

it didnt include anyone on it dat you cd in

Ishmael Reed / **133**

vite to a cocktail party & shoot a lot of
            bull   right ?
so you want to take it out on my hide right ?
well i got news for you professor nothing - i
am my own brand while you must be d fantasy of
        a japanese cartoonist
a strangekind of dinosaurmouse
i can see it all now . d leaves
are running low . its d eve of
extinction & dere are no holes'to
accept yr behind . you wander abt yr
long neck probing a tree . you think
its a tree but its really a trap . a
cry of victory goes up in d kitchen of
d world . a pest is dead . a prehis
toric pest at dat . a really funnytime
prehistoric pest whom we will lug into
a museum to show everyone how really funny
you are   yr fate wd make a good
scenario but d plot is between you &
charles darwin . you know, white folkses
            business

as i said . im passing thru . just sing
ing my song . get along little doggie &
jazz like dat . word has it dat a big gold
shipment is coming to californy . i hv to
ride all night if im to meet my pardners
dey want me to help score d ambush

Beware : Do Not Read This Poem

tonite, thriller was
abt an ol woman, so vain she
surrounded herself w/
   many mirrors

it got so bad that finally she
locked herself indoors & her
whole life became the
    mirrors

one day the villagers broke
into her house , but she was too
swift for them . she disappeared
    into a mirror
each tenant who bought the house
after that , lost a loved one to
    the ol woman in the mirror :
    first a little girl
    then a young woman
    then the young woman/s husband

the hunger of this poem is legendary
it has taken in many victims
back off from this poem
it has drawn in yr feet
back off from this poem
it has drawn in yr legs

back off from this poem
it is a greedy mirror
you are into this poem . from
    the waist down
nobody can hear you can they ?
this poem has had you up to here
      belch
this poem aint got no manners
you cant call out frm this poem
relax now & go w/ this poem

move & roll on to this poem
do not resist this poem
this poem has yr eyes
this poem has his head
this poem has his arms
this poem has his fingers
this poem has his fingertips

this poem is the reader & the
reader this poem

statistic : the us bureau of missing persons reports
            that in 1968 over 100,000 people disappeared
            leaving no solid clues
                          nor trace   only
      a space   in the lives of their friends

About The Poets

Al Young

Al Young says of himself:

"Born 1939 at Ocean Springs, Mississippi near Biloxi. Spent childhood shuttling between southern & northern U.S. Started writing westerns, detectives & science fictions in notebooks around age 10. Began to 2-finger type in the 6th grade & turned out my own hectographed comic weekly mag *The Krazy Krazette* in jr. high. Lived in a world of nutty friends, music, library books & school publications before joining staff of *Idioms*, a publication of the New Music Society, Detroit, in 1956, edited by black painter Harold Neal & his wife. Contributed articles & poetry before being accepted on a trial basis by the Univ. of Mich. In college played guitar & sang for wages in coffeehouses; also co-edited the lit mag *Generation*, going sleepless as always to write stories, poems, confessions, journals. Left Michigan in 1961 to wander & see the sad world. Came west, went to Mexico, went to Europe. Worked as musician, disk jockey, yard clerk for the S.P. & countless other occupations. Took a degree at U.C. Berkeley in Spanish. Founded & still edit *Loveletter.* Have published poetry & prose in innumerable magazines & reviews. Awarded Stegner Writing Fellowship, 1966–67 & the Joseph Henry Jackson Award, 1969–70. Taught at San Francisco Museum of Art, Neighborhood Youth Corps & Stanford. Have written a novel (SNAKES) which is acquiring an underground following in manuscript. DANCING, a collection of poetry, published by Corinth Books, New York. Poetry is for me essentially a spiritual activity, man being an infinitely expressive being. We have already entered the era in which soul must play a more important role on Earth than body."

Mr. Young's prose and poetry has been published in quarterlies and small magazines throughout the U.S. and also in Mexico and India including, *Massachusetts Review, El Corno Emplumado, Black Dialogue, Perspectives, Galley Sail Review, Guerrilla, Work, Camels Coming, Journal of Black Poetry, The Lit* (Notre Dame), *Spero, Aldebaran Review, Journal for the Protection of All Beings, Alpha Sort, Black on Black.*

DeLeon Harrison

Writer, Film-maker, Painter. Born in Little Rock, Arkansas, traveled extensively, came to California as a teenager. Instructor at San Francisco State College in English and Jazz History. Co-founder and Director of Seshesh Media Workshop (Drama, Dance, Poetry, Film-making, Music). Co-founder of Cinema Blackscope. Commentator for KPFA fm (Inside on the Outside—Avante-Garde Jazz). Currently residing in Berkeley California where he is doing research in the field of Psycho-Linguistics. Play—"Poetry of the Revolution" to be produced by Seshesh.

One of DeLeon Harrison's many interests is in using media and kinesthetic forms to create poetry and give it the sense of immediacy he feels our times demand. "Yellow" is barely suggestive; a conductor's notes. "Yellow" is not written to be printed, but to be performed. It is included here to indicate one of the directions the poet is working in. Following the conductor's notes, the reader may make his own poem.

His poems have appeared in *Black Dialogue* and *Axolotl*, and are produced by Seshesh.

Sarah Webster Fabio

Sarah Webster Fabio is a woman of many lives. In addition to being a wife and mother of five children, she finds time to teach, lecture and read her works, traveling widely to do each. She has taught Afro literature and drama or lectured and conducted workshops at Fisk University, Merritt College, Cornell University, Cazenovia College, and University of California at Berkeley. A frequent contributor to *Negro Digest*, her work has also appeared in *College Composition and Communication*. Her two-part volume of poems, *A Mirror: A Soul* is published by Success Books, 1969.

Calvin C. Hernton

Calvin Hernton is a poet, sociologist, novelist. A graduate of Talledega and Fisk Universities, he did study toward a doctorate in sociology at Columbia University and has taught sociology at several colleges. His books include: *Sex and Racism in America,* Evergreen 1965, *White Papers for White Americans,* 1966, and a book of poetry, *The Coming of Chronos to the House of Nightsong.* His poems have appeared in such publications as *Umbra* and *The New Black Poetry,* 1969, edited by Clarence Major.

Victor Hernandez Cruz

Victor Hernandez Cruz says of himself:

"I was born in Aguas Buenas, a small village in Boriquen (Indian name for Puerto Rico). My family split P.R. when I was 4 years old and I've been in N.Y. ever since. My poems have appeared in *Evergreen Review, Ramparts, For/Now, Down Here, Umbra, Journal of Black Poetry.* Random House published *Snaps* (1969), a book of poems. I'm currently working on a novel."

Doing Poetry is a broadside by Victor Hernandez Cruz, published by Other Ways, Berkeley, California, 1968.

conyus

conyus is living and working in San Francisco. A book of his poems is being considered by a major publisher.

Lucille Clifton

Lucille Clifton says of herself:

"I am 33 years old, married and have six children. Before this year I had had only one poem published, in *Negro Digest.* Publishing has seemed less important than writing and I hadn't thought about it very much. I majored in Drama at Howard University a long time ago but dropped out. My family is my first thing and everything else is second. I love to read good things to people. First book published in 1969 by Random House. Two children's books to be published by Holt."

Mrs. Clifton is a recipient of the Discovery '69 award. The poems included in this selection appeared in *The Massachusetts Review* (Winter, 1969).

A. B. Spellman

A. B. Spellman is a poet, historian and jazz critic. His poetry and jazz criticism have appeared in such magazines as, *The Nation, The New Republic, Metronome, The Liberator, Black Dialogue, Umbra* and *The Journal of Black Poetry.* His *Four Lives in the Bebop Business* (1966) gives insight into the careers of Ornette Coleman, Herbie Nichols, Jackie McLean and Cecil Taylor.

His varied activities have included managing a bookstore and conducting a radio program on jazz and ethnic music. Along with LeRoi Jones and Larry Neal, he is an editor of *The Cricket,* a journal of Black music. He has been writer in residence at Morehouse College and Emory University, Atlanta.

The poems included in *Dices* are from *The Beautiful Days,* Poets Press (1965), with the exception of "when black people are . . ." and "in orangeburg my brothers did . . . ," which first appeared in *The Journal of Black Poetry* (Fall 1968).

N. H. Pritchard

N. H. Pritchard was born in New York City in 1939. He attended The Cathedral Choir School of St. John the Divine and St. Peter's School (Jacob's Hill) before receiving his Bachelor of Arts degree with Honors in Art History from Washington Square College, New York University. While attending college he was a contributor to the literary magazine and President of the Fine Arts Society. His poems have appeared in many periodicals, including, *Poetry Northwest, Liberator, Eye Magazine, Umbra* and *The East Village Other.* He has read his poems on the record albums: *Destinations: Four Contemporary American Poets* and *New Jazz Poets.* Mr. Pritchard is currently teaching a poetry workshop at The New School for Social Research and is Poet in Residence at Friends Seminary. He is the author of *The Matrix: Poems 1960–1970* (Doubleday) and is at present working on a novel.

Etheridge Knight

Of himself Mr. Knight says: "I died in Korea from a shrapnel wound and narcotics resurrected me. I died in 1960 from a prison sentence and poetry brought me back to life." Etheridge Knight has published stories and poems in *Negro Digest, Journal of Black Poetry* and other periodicals. The poems in *Dices* are taken from *Poems from Prison,* by Broadside Press.

William Anderson

William Anderson says that the only relevant biographical material about himself is that he is a poet, journalist and novelist.

"The February Rain is Falling" first appeared in *The San Francisco Bay Guardian.*

David Henderson

David Henderson was born in Harlem in 1942. He has lived in Greenwich Village, Acapulco, San Francisco and New Orleans. He was first published in *The Black American.* His collections of poetry are: *Felix of the Silent Forest,* Poets Press, 1967 and *De Mayor of Harlem,* E.P. Dutton, 1970. He lectured at City College of New York, 1967–68, was Poet-in-residence at CCNY, Fall 1969, worked with the Free Southern Theater, summer 1967, and is consultant to colleges and universities. He is editor and founding editor of *Umbra Anthology*. His poems have appeared in numerous publications and anthologies.

Patricia Parker

Texas-born Patricia Parker has published in such periodicals as *Loveletter* and *Black Dialogue*. A Berkeley resident, she has read her works throughout the San Francisco Bay area.

Adam David Miller

Adam David Miller was born and spent his life through high school in Orangeburg, South Carolina. About it, he says: "When I was young, they just ran you out of town. Today they shoot you."
He is an Instructor of English at Laney College, Oakland, where he teaches Afro literature and composition, and heads the Tutoring Service. In 1964 he helped found The Aldridge Players/West, a San Francisco Afro drama group, and since that time he has served variously as production coordinator, actor and director; he is chairman of the board of directors. He has lectured and conducted seminars on Afro literature, especially poetry and drama, both locally and throughout the U.S. He is an S.F. Bay Area correspondent for *Black Theatre* and has written articles on Afro theatre and literature for several periodicals, including *The Drama Review* and *The S.F. Chronicle*. He is a founding editor of *The Graduate Student Journal,* a magazine of opinion, at the University of California at Berkeley, from which institution he holds an M.A. in English.

A career teacher, his interests are in individual and small group instruction, the prevention of Black cultural genocide, and human survival via Ecology Action.

Clarence Major

Clarence Major is one of the country's most productive young writers. Though only 32, his work has been published widely in literary and poetry journals in this country, Canada, India, Brazil and Mexico. His novel, *The All-Night Visitors* and an anthology, *The New Black Poetry* were published in 1969, and scheduled for 1970 publication are: *Three Literary Giants: Wright, Baldwin, Williams, Biographies* and *Dictionary of Afro-American Slang*. He has edited his own literary journal, has served as associate editor of others, and as a contributing editor of *The Journal of Black Poetry*. He has also been a contributor to several anthologies. *The Sounds of My Eyes*, a collection of his poetry, is also scheduled for publication.

He was born in Atlanta, Georgia, and lives and teaches in New York City.

Glenn Myles

Glenn Myles was born in Carthage, Texas in 1933. He majored in illustration at California College of Arts and Crafts. In addition to calendar, poster, and book illustrations, he has written poetry and short stories. "Percy/68" first appeared in *Uhuru* (1968) and was reprinted in *The New Black Poetry*, edited by Clarence Major (1969).

He is the illustrator for *Dices*.

Ishmael Reed

Ishmael Reed is the most exciting novelist in the U.S. His *Freelance Pallbearers* (1968) is enjoying an enthusiastic response in this country and is being promoted by a growing list of foreign publishers. He is also a university lecturer. Most recently, he has conducted classes on contemporary fiction at the University of Washington (Seattle), Spring 1969 and the University of California at Berkeley, Spring 1968 and 1969.

His poetry has been published widely in periodicals and anthologies, and a collection of his poems, *Catechism of the Neo-American Hoodoo Church*, is scheduled for publication in England. He is the editor of an anthology of excerpts from contemporary novels, *Fifteen Necromancers From Now*, to be published in 1970. His newest novel, *Yellow Back Radio Broke Down* (1969), the story of Loop Garou, the hoodoo cowboy, can only add to what is a growing literary reputation. Ishmael Reed was one of the founders of *The East Village Other*. He is currently at work on a hoodoo detective novel. "I Am A Cowboy In The Boat Of Ra" first appeared in *The New Black Poetry*, edited by Clarence Major (1969).

Of his writing, he says simply, "I try to do what has never been done before."